HUMAN RIGHTS VIOLATIONS AND PEACEFUL PROTESTS IN THE REPUBLIC OF GUINEA

Friki Camara

Published by New Generation Publishing in 2024

First Edition

ISBN: 978-1-83563-242-0

www.newgeneration-publishing.com

New Generation Publishing

Dedication

This Book is dedicated to all those Young People who were killed by Military bullets during peaceful protests in the Republic of Guinea, in Africa and the wide world. May they Rest in Peace.

Preface

The entire world has 195 countries out of which 110 have experienced a peaceful demonstration at one point in their history. Peaceful demonstrations are organized to vent out citizens' grievances that arise from the authorities' negligence for responsiveness. Essentially, why government and stakeholders have geared efforts towards curtailing human rights violations of citizens, which seem not to be enough; and the reason for which peaceful demonstrations are staged, there is need to investigate whether these peaceful demonstrations can have an impact on the reduction of human rights violations in The Republic of Guinea.

The work discovered that it is the human rights violations and abuse that prompt peaceful demonstrations. Therefore, it is recommended that in order to ensure that peaceful demonstrations have a better impact on the reduction of human rights violations, the flow of communication between peaceful demonstrators or protesters should be enhanced through advocacies and public awareness campaigns, which could be done by bills or jingles broadcast on radio and televisions stations across the country.

The use of violence and the killing of demonstrators to disperse ongoing protests and ending of arbitrary arrest of human rights defenders and peaceful demonstrators as well as unlawful detention should be discouraged by the strengthening of political will to enforce global and domesticated human rights treaties or laws. There should be a provision of a policy to allow freedom of media or press during peaceful demonstrations or protests, which will promote the ending of ethnic fractioning and prevention of the involvement of security forces that do not have the mandate to exercise crowd control who unlawfully use teargas and rubber bullets to dispel peaceful demonstrators and perpetrate physical aggression, torture, forced disappearance and murder.

Friki Camara
Northern Ireland, Belfast, United Kingdom

Foreword

The frugality we enjoyed was astonishingly appealing that we couldn't allow our intellects to wallow in mendicant indolence to fuse our dignity into mediocrity and adduced futility. One wish kept us trying as the Tiv people and Africans; and it was never to be like the British or French Colonialists but to acquaint ourselves with civilization on our own terms. Colonialism itself was occasioned by purported human rights violations embellished with Coercion, Racketeering and Banditry crowned in Terrorism, which the same purveyors are condemning today.

Apparently, since the advent of colonialism in Africa, the continent has been ominously plagued by human rights violations precipitated on the frontiers of usurpation of economic resources and heritages. Colonialism surreptitiously stole the African Ubuntu and communality that bounded them to the creeds that fostered love and benevolence. Regrettably, across the African climes, The Republic of Guinea, with a once peaceful and humane ambience has turned out to be one of the most porous nations for human rights violations where peaceful protest and demonstrations aimed at curtailing the excesses of perpetrators of human rights violations is truncated by authorities and allies.

The flamboyant author of this book "HUMAN RIGHTS VIOLATIONS AND PEACEFUL PROTEST IN THE REPUBLIC OF GUINEA" has been lavishly democratic in most liberal manner to not only frown at the upsurge of human rights violations in his dear country but also attune the reader with approaches to improve peaceful demonstrations and reduction of human rights violations in The Republic of Guinea to such an ambrosia and timely innings that must be appreciated with solemn gratitude.

Essentially, this book is divided into four chapters, including the Emergence of Conakry, Problem of Human

Rights Violations, Conceptualization of Human Rights Violations and Peaceful Demonstration and Analytical Discourse, which ends with conclusions and recommendations. The author Monsieur Friki Camara has conscientiously delved into advancing the frontiers of knowledge in human rights violations and how peaceful protests or demonstrations can help reduce it and brought to our doorsteps. This is a wonderful book that I humbly recommend to be read in schools, colleges, and universities across the country and elsewhere in the world. Those studying Governance and Human Rights, Peace Studies and Conflict Resolutions among others can find this book very useful in their respective areas.

Tim Cuttings Agber
International research consultant
Department of library and information science
Benue state university Makurdy Nigeria
Abuja ,Nigeria 5th November 2023

Acknowledgements

In the course of my academic pursuits and social interactions, I have met with numerous people who have been of tremendous assistance to me and my family who I cannot, for want of time and space mention here all; but let me first acknowledge my parents Elhadj Bandjougou Camara and Hadja Fanta Conde, Souayibatou Kante, Bachir Junior Camara, Khadija Camara, Fatima Fifi Camara, Aboubacar Sidiki Camara, Elhadj Fanta Brema camara and brothers.

My friends Theresa Theune and Family, Ruth Gray Simon Coulter and Family,Moira Mc Combe and family, Koman Doumbouya, Fode Sacko Defo. Sabine Preuss and family, Auntie Cho Gervaise & tonton jean jacques kouakou, Tantie Desiree & Narcisse koudou .

LIST OF ABBREVIATIONS

ACHPR	African Charter on Human and Peoples' Rights
AHRC	Australian Human Rights Commission
AIPDRHRVQ	Assessment of the Impact of Peaceful Demonstration on Reduction of Human Rights Violations Questionnaire
AU	African Union
BRB	Repression of Banditry Brigade
COVID	Corona Virus Disease
ECOWAS	Economic Community of Western African States
EU	European Union
FEWER	Forum on Early Warning and Early Response
FGM	Female Genital Mutilation
FNDC	Front National pour la Défense de la Constitution
HRW	Human Rights Watch
KELHRVQ	Knowledge of Education Law and Human Rights Violations Questionnaire
NVR	Non-Violent Resistance
OAU	Organization of African Union
OHCHR	Office of the United Nations High Commissioner for Human Rights
RAA	Reasoned Action Approach
RDA	Rassemblement Democratique Africain
RFI	Radio France International
RPG	Rally of the Guinean People
SARS	Special Anti-Robbery Squad
TAT	Tiv Anchôgholuv Theory
TLP	Tournons la Page-Guinea
ToRA	Theory of Reasoned Action
TPB	Theory of Planned Behavior
TRA	Theory of Reasoned Action
UDHR	Universal Declaration of Human Rights

UN	The United Nations
UNDP	The United Nations Development Programme
UNESCO	The United Nations Educational, Scientific and Cultural Organization
WANEP	West African Network for Peace-Building

Table of Contents

Dedication -- iii

Preface-- iv

Foreword-- vi

Acknowledgements --- viii

LIST OF ABBREVIATIONS ---------------------------- ix

Table of Contents-- xi

CHAPTER ONE-- 1

The Emergence of Conakry ----------------------------------- 1

The Regions --- 6

Guinea National Anthem -------------------------------------- 8

Liberté-- 8

GREAT WRITERS --------------------------------------- 10

Camara Laye --- 10

Fodéba Keïta --- 11

Ahmed Sékou Touré -------------------------------------- 13

Kesso Barry--- 15

Koumanthio Zeinab Diallo------------------------------- 16

Saïdou Bokoum -- 18

Tierno Monénembo -- 19

CHAPTER TWO -- 23

Problem of Human Rights Violations ------------------- 23

Paramount Duty of Government ------------------------- 24

Why Human Rights Violations and Peaceful Protests-28

CHAPTER THREE --30

Conceptualization of Human Rights Violations and Peaceful Demonstrations -----------------------------------30

Peaceful Demonstrations and Reduction of Human Rights Violations ---36

Factors Militating against Peaceful Demonstrations and Reduction of Human Rights Violations------------------40

Strategies Adopted to Improve Peaceful Demonstrations and Reduction of Human Rights Violations-------------44

Theoretical Considerations----------------------------------45

Theory of Reasoned Action---------------------------------47

The Tiv Anchôgholuv Theory------------------------------53

Review of Related Studies ---------------------------------56

CHAPTER FOUR---59

Analytical Discourse ---------------------------------------59

Types of Human Rights Violations in The Republic of Guinea---59

Human Rights Violations that Prompt Peaceful Demonstration or Protest in the Republic of Guinea---60

Challenges of Peaceful Demonstrations and Reduction of Human Rights Violations in the Republic of Guinea --61

Approaches to Improve Peaceful Demonstrations and Reduction of Human Rights Violations in the Republic of Guinea --62

Conclusion--63

Recommendations -- 64

Bibliography-- 66

CHAPTER ONE

The Emergence of Conakry

French Guinea is what is today known as the Republic of Guinea and it used to be a French Colony, a nation that got its independence on 2 October 1958. The country's headquarters is located in Conakry, founded in 1884 on Tombo Island when the French settlers invaded the locality, which belonged to the Susu or Soussou people. The political struggles over who rules Conakry were a dispute that was stifled in 1890 and it lasted until Great Britain officially ceded the island to France. The locality was named *Guinée Française* by 1895 and eventually, Conakry became the capital of French Guinea in 1904 and was the seaport terminus of the only railroad in the French Colony. According to Brooks (1999), Darboe (2010) and Lewis (2014):

The word "Guinea" came into use among European shippers and map makers in the seventeenth century to refer to the coast of West Africa from Guinea to Benin. Some Guineans claim that the word arose from an early episode in the European-African encounter. In Susu, the language spoken by the coastal Susu ethnic group, the word guinè means "woman". When a group of Europeans arrived on the coast, they met some women washing clothes in an estuary. The women indicated to the men that they were women. The Europeans misunderstood and thought the women were referring to a geographic area; they subsequently used the word "Guinea" to describe coastal West Africa. After Guinea gained independence, the first president, Sekou Touré, named the country the People's Revolutionary Republic of Guinea. The second president, Lansana Conté, changed the official name to the Republic of Guinea. The capital city is Conakry, and the country often is referred to as Guinea-Conakry to distinguish it from other nation-states with the same name. Conakry is divided into quarters with a number of large tree-lined boulevards inspired by Paris and other French cities. Originally the city was only on Tombo Island but has since expanded to include the Iles de Los and the Kaloum Peninsula, which is connected to Tombo Island by a causeway.

The larger populations of Guineans live in rural communities and speak more than thirty languages of the various tribes, and eight of the languages are designated as official national languages. Bah and Sienta (2022) reported that about 67 per cent of Guineans live in rural areas. Most are subsistence farmers on very small plots. About 63 per cent of rural people are poor, twice the rate in urban areas.

Productivity is low because farmers have little access to information, new technologies, basic infrastructure or rural financial services. Rural dwellers have few ways to earn except farming, and availability of healthcare, education and safe drinking water is very limited in rural areas. Developing agricultural value chains in Guinea is very difficult, because institutions and the regulatory framework are weak, government services work badly, basic infrastructure is inadequate and there are too few rural finance institutions.

The territory that is now the Republic of Guinea was part of succeeding empires of West Africa, historically referred to as the Empires of the Western Sudan, existing between the tenth and fifteenth centuries. The Republic of Guinea has had a turbulent political history. After rejecting Imperial France's Loi Cadre, Guinea declared independence on 2 October 1958, two years earlier than other francophone countries in Africa. Loi Cadre, enacted in France in 1956 after tremendous pressure from its colonies, transferred considerable administrative powers to the colonies, but fell far short of the independence most Africans had asked for. For example, under Loi Cadre France continued to control foreign affairs, currency, and economic matters. Consequently, Guineans held a referendum and decisively voted against any further French colonial rule, feeling that accession to Loi Cadre would position Guinea as a "junior partner" to France. The "No" vote was orchestrated by the Guinea branch of the Rassemblement Democratique Africain (African Democratic Rally [RDA]), an "inter-territorial movement of political parties and groups in Francophone countries in West and Central Africa". By 1958, the Guinea branch had become radical and driven by pressures from the grassroots, and it defied the position of the RDA in other French West African territories and voted for immediate independence and made Ahmed Sekou Toure (commonly referred to as Sekou Toure) its first president (Darboe, 2010).

In the narrations of Internet Archive (1998), Diallo and Nossiter (2010), Samb (2013), Dinerstein, Olson, Joshi, Vynne, Burgess, Wikramanayake, Hahn, Palminteri, Hedao, Noss, Hansen, Locke, Ellis, Jones, Barber, Hayes, Kormos, Martin, Crist, Sechrest, Price, Baillie, Weeden, Suckling, Davis, Sizer, Moore, Thau, Birch, Potapov, Turubanova, Tyukavina, de Souza, Pintea, Brito, Llewellyn, Miller, Patzelt, Ghazanfar, Timberlake, Klöser, Shennan-Farpón, Kindt, Lillesø, van Breugel, Graudal, Voge, Al-Shammari and Saleem (2017:535), Grantham, Duncan, Evans, Jones, Beyer, Schuster, Walston, Ray, Robinson, Callow, Clements, Costa, DeGemmis, Elsen, Ervin, Franco, Goldman, Goetz, Hansen, Hofsvang, Jantz, Jupiter, Kang, Langhammer, Laurance, Lieberman, Linkie, Malhi, Maxwell, Mendez, Mittermeier, Murray, Possingham, Radachowsky, Saatchi, Samper, Silverman, Shapiro, Strassburg, Stevens, Stokes, Taylor, Tear, Tizard, Venter, Visconti, Wang and Watson (2020:3), Paquett and Timsit (2021), Larson (2021) and One World - Nations Online (2022) reported that:

Guinea is a republic. The president is directly elected by the people and is the head of state and the head of government. The unicameral National Assembly is the legislative body of the country, and its members are directly elected by the people. The judicial branch is headed by the Supreme Court of Guinea, the highest and final court of appeal in the country. The National Assembly of Guinea, the country's legislative body, did not meet from 2008 to 2013, when it was dissolved after the military coup in December. Elections have been postponed multiple times since 2007. In April 2012, President Condé postponed the elections indefinitely, citing the need to ensure that they were "transparent and democratic". The 2013 Guinean legislative election was held on 24

September. President Alpha Condé's party, the Rally of the Guinean People (RPG), won a plurality of seats in the National Assembly of Guinea, with 53 out of 114 seats. The opposition parties won a total of 53 seats, and opposition leaders denounced the official results as fraudulent. Guinea is divided into 4 regions: Maritime Guinea, also known as Lower Guinea or the Basse-Coté lowlands, populated mainly by the Susu ethnic group; the cooler, more mountainous Fouta Djallon that run roughly north–south through the middle of the country, populated by Fulas; the Sahelian Haute-Guinea to the northeast, populated by Malinké; and the forested jungle regions in the southeast, with several ethnic groups.

Guinea's mountains are the source for the Niger, the Gambia, and Senegal Rivers, and rivers flowing to the sea on the west side of the range in Sierra Leone and Ivory Coast. The highest point in Guinea is Mount Nimba at 1,752 m (5,748 ft). While the Guinean and Ivorian sides of the Nimba Massif are a UNESCO Strict Nature Reserve, the portion of the so-called Guinean Backbone continues into Liberia, where it has been mined for decades; the damage is evident in the Nzérékoré Region at 7°32'17"N 8°29'50"W. Guinea is home to 5 ecoregions: Guinean montane forests, Western Guinean lowland forests, Guinean forest-savanna mosaic, West Sudanian savanna, and Guinean mangroves. It had a 2019 Forest Landscape Integrity Index mean score of 4.9/10, ranking it 114th globally out of 172 countries.

Essentially, the rural communities in The Republic of Guinea are inhabited by the country's tribesmen including Mandinka, Fulani, Soussou, Kissi, Kpelle, Toma and they speak Bassari, Guerzé, Kissi, Koniagui, Maninka, Peul,

Susu, and Toma languages among others. Moreover, most of these tribes are involved in cultural practices such as blacksmithing, basket making, weaving, and other cultural practices. World Atlas (2022) affirm cultural practices among the Soussou and other rural community aborigines noting that Mandinkas are subsistence farmers who rely on millet, maize, and rice; and villages are autonomous led by a chief. Kankaung is a rite of passage which marks the beginning of adulthood.

The Regions

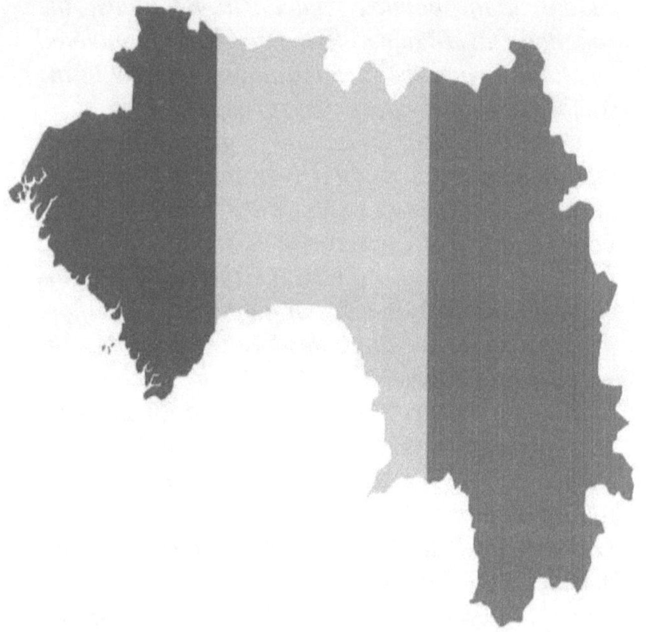

The Republic of Guinea has eight regions, which are Boké Region, Conakry Region, Faranah Region, Kankan Region, Kindia Region, Labé Region, Mamou Region and Nzérékoré Region. Importantly, the Republic of Guinea is a country where human rights violations are paramount (Rédaction Africanews, 2022) and incessant peaceful demonstrations continue to rise (Human Rights Watch,

2022) with the hope of curtailing the human rights abuses or violations (Radio France International – RFI, 2022) for the survival and peaceful coexistence of the citizens.

The Republic of Guinea's population can be found by regions and prefectures as presented in the table below.

Table 1: Populations at Recent Censuses of Conakry Special Zone and the 33 Prefectures

SN	Name	Area (km²)	Census 1983 (4 Feb)	Census 1996 (1 Dec)	Census 2014 (1 March)	Administrative Capital
	Région de Conakry	450	710,372	1,092,936	1,667,864	
1	Conakry	450	710,372	1,092,936	1,667,864	Conakry
	Région de Boké	31,186	508,724	760,119	1,081,445	
2	Boffa	5,050	113,981	156,558	211,063	Boffa
3	Boké	11,124	168,924	293,917	449,405	Boké
4	Fria	2,016	52,908	81,790	96,527	Fria
5	Gaoual	7,758	103,516	137,624	194,245	Gaoual
6	Koundara	5,238	69,395	90,230	130,205	Koundara
	Région de Faranah	35,581	425,160	602,845	942,733	
7	Dabola	6,350	73,937	111,363	182,951	Dabola
8	Dinguiraye	7,965	99,363	137,380	195,662	Dinguiraye
9	Faranah	12,966	109,104	147,347	280,511	Faranah
10	Kissidougou	8,300	142,756	206,755	283,609	Kissidougou
	Région de Kankan	72,145	640,432	1,011,644	1,986,329	
11	Kankan	19,750	172,767	262,350	472,112	Kankan
12	Kérouané	7,020	87,040	154,861	211,017	Kérouané
13	Kouroussa	14,050	107,741	150,059	268,224	Kouroussa
14	Mandiana	12,825	111,671	173,150	339,527	Mandiana
15	Siguiri	18,500	161,303	271,224	695,449	Siguiri
	Région de Kindia	28,873	555,937	928,312	1,559,185	
16	Coyah	1,275	116,840	85,148	264,164	Coyah
17	Dubréka	4,350	-	131,337	328,418	Dubréka
18	Forécariah	4,384	90,403	195,836	244,649	Forécariah
19	Kindia	9,648	163,032	287,611	438,315	Kindia
20	Télimélé	9,216	185,662	228,380	283,639	Télimélé
	Région de Labé	22,869	642,617	799,545	995,717	

21	Koubia	3,725	70,715	91,882	101,171	Koubia
22	Labé	2,242	185,594	251,702	318,633	Labé
23	Lélouma	4,275	121,079	137,273	162,634	Lélouma
24	Mali	8,802	184,936	204,041	290,320	Mali
25	Tougué	3,825	80,293	114,647	122,959	Tougué
	Région de Mamou	17,074	437,212	612,218	732,117	
26	Dalaba	3,328	96,571	136,656	136,320	Dalaba
27	Mamou	9,108	139,764	236,326	318,738	Mamou
28	Pita	4,638	200,877	239,236	277,059	Pita
	Région de Nzérékoré	37,658	740,128	1,348,787	1,663,582	
29	Beyla	13,612	120,610	169,730	325,482	Beyla
30	Guéckédou	4,750	150,997	347,541	291,823	Guéckédou
31	Lola	4,688	76,689	134,326	175,213	Lola
32	Macenta	7,056	142,355	278,789	298,282	Macenta
33	Nzérékoré	3,632	194,600	283,413	396,118	Nzérékoré
34	Yomou	3,920	54,877	134,988	176,664	Yomou
	Total Guinea	245,836	4,660,582	7,156,406	10,628,972	

Guinea National Anthem
Liberté

Peuple d'Afrique,
Le Passé historique!
Que chante l'hymne de la Guinée fière et jeune
Illustre épopée de nos frères
Morts au champ d'honneur en libérant l'Afrique!
Le peuple de Guinée prêchant l'unité
Appelle l'Afrique.
Liberté! C'est la voix d'un peuple
Qui appelle tous ses frères de la grande Afrique.
Liberté! C'est la voix d'un peuple
Qui appelle tous ses frères à se retrouver.
Bâtissons l'unité africaine dans l'indépendance retrouvée.

Freedom

People of Africa!
The historic past!
Sing the hymn of a Guinea proud and young
Illustrious epic of our brothers
Who died on the field of honor while liberating Africa!
The people of Guinea, preaching Unity,
Call to Africa.
Liberty! The voice of a people
Who call all her brothers of a great Africa.
Liberty! The voice of a people
Who call all her brothers to find their way again.
Let us build African Unity in a newly found independence!

GREAT WRITERS

Camara Laye

Camara Laye was a writer from Guinea. He was the author of *L'Enfant noir* or *The African Child* (1953), a novel based loosely on his own childhood, and *The Radiance of the King* (1954). Both novels are among the earliest major works in Francophone African literature, and in 1980, Camara Laye published *The Guardian of the Word*.

Camara Laye was born in the Kouroussa town of the French Guinea on 1 January 1928 in what is today the Republic of Guinea, and he died in the City of Dakar, Senegal on 4 February 1980.

Fodéba Keïta

Fodéba Keïta was born on 19 January 1921 in Siguiri, French Guinea in what is today known as The Republic of Guinea. He was a man of multiple skills and vocations. In his lifetime, he was a playwright, dancer, writer, musician, politician and composer. Apparently, Fodéba died on 27 May 1969 when he was shot dead at Camp Boiro.

Conteh-Morgan (1994) reported that Keita was the founder of the first professional African theatrical troupe, Theatre Africain, and he also arranged *Liberté*, the national anthem of Guinea. According to Charry (2000), Onwudiwe (2003) and Banham (2004), Fodéba Keïta founded the band "Sud Jazz" in 1948 during his law studies in Paris, and beginning in the late 1940s, he founded Théâtre Africain, which was later known as Les Ballets Africains, which was a successful ballet group that toured Africa for six years and later became the national dance company of Guinea. President of Senegal Léopold Sédar Senghor held it in high esteem; with Kanté Facély and Les Ballets Africains, Fodéba became instrumental in showcasing previously unknown Mandé performance traditions to other continents.

Eventually, when Fodéba returned to Guinea, he published the poetry collection *Poèmes africains* in 1950; another novel *Le Maître d'école* in 1952, and in 1957, he wrote and staged the narrative poem *Aube africaine* or *African Dawn* as a theatre-ballet based on the Thiaroye massacre. In *African Dawn*, a young man called Naman complies with the French colonial rulers by fighting in the French Army only to be killed in Thiaroye in Senegal, in a dispute between West-African soldiers and white officers. However, his works were banned in French Africa as he was considered radical and anticolonial (Miller, 1990; Esonwanne, 1993; Banham, Hill & Woodyard, 1994; O'Toole & Baker, 2005; Falola & Ter Haar, 2010).

Hudgens and Trillo (2003); O'Toole, and Baker (2005) asserted that Fodéba was politically active in the African Democratic Rally and worked closely with Sékou Touré, the country's first president who was himself a writer from 1956, and in 1957 was elected to the Territorial Assembly. In 1961, he was appointed minister for defense and security. He uncovered alleged plots against Sékou Touré, but was imprisoned in the infamous Camp Boiro, a prison he himself helped construct, for alleged complicity in February 1969 Labé Plot, and was subjected to torture "diète noire".

Ahmed Sékou Touré

The Guinean political leader and African statesman Ahmed Sékou Touré was the first president of Guinea who served his country from 1958 to 1984. He was born on the 9 January 1922 and was among the principal Guinean nationalists who were involved in gaining independence of the country from the French Colonial Government.

Pace (1984) and Schmidt, (2007) submitted that Sékou Touré died of an apparent heart attack on 26 March 1984 while undergoing cardiac treatment in the United States of America at the Cleveland Clinic in Cleveland, Ohio, for emergency heart surgery. Touré was struck in the Saudi Arabia and was flown to the United States and when he died, he was buried at the Camayanne Mausoleum, located inside the gardens of the Grand Mosque of Conakry in the Republic of Guinea. Essentially, some of the works by the great Ahmed Sékou Touré include the following:

- Ahmed Sékou Touré (1983). *Guinée-Festival / commentaire et montage, Wolibo Dukuré dit Grand-*

pére. Conakry: Commission Culturelle du Comité Central.

- Ahmed Sékou Touré (1979). *Political leader considered as the representative of a culture.* Newark, N.J.: Jihad Productions.
- Ahmed Sékou Touré (1978). *Strategy and tactics of the revolution*. Conakry, Guinea: Press Office.
- Ahmed Sékou Touré (1975). *Hommage à la révolution Cubaine; Message du camarade Ahmed Sekou Toure au peuple Cubain à l'occasion du 20ᵉ anniversaire de l'attaque de la Caserne de Moncada (Juillet 1973)*. Conakry: Bureau de Presse de la Presidence de la Republique.
- Ahmed Sékou Touré (1973). *Afrika and imperialism.* Newark, N.J.: Jihad Productions Company.
- Ahmed Sékou Touré (1972). *Pour l'amitié algéro-guinéenne*. Conakry, Guinea: Parti démocratique de Guinée.
- Ahmed Sékou Touré (1971). *Address of President Ahmed Sékou Touré, President of the Republic of Guinee [sic]: suggestions submitted during the West Africa consultative regional meeting held at Conakry, during 19 and 20 November 1971.* Cairo: Permanent Secretariat of the Afro-Asian Peoples' Solidarity Organization.
- Ahmed Sékou Touré (1964). *Poèmes militants.* Conakry, Guinea: Parti démocratique de Guinée.
- Ahmed Sékou Touré (1962). *International policy and diplomatic action of the Democratic Party of Guinea; extracts from the report on doctrine and orientation submitted to the 3d National Conference of the P.D.G.* Cairo: Société Orientale de Publicité-Press.
- Ahmed Sékou Touré (1958). *Guinée, prélude à l'indépendance (Avant-propos de Jacques Rabemananjara)* Paris: Présence africaine.

Kesso Barry

Kesso Barry was born in 1948 and her works include Kesso, princesse peuhle (Kesso, a Fulani princess), which was published in 1988 in Paris, France by Seghers. Sankara (2011) and Bekers (2012) reported that Kesso is a Guinean autobiographical writer who writes in French. Her autobiography, dedicated to her daughter, recounts the restrictive gender roles of her traditional upbringing as a member of the Fulani nobility in Guinea, and her escape to a Westernized life in Paris.

Apparently, O'Toole and Baker (2005) noted that Kesso Barry's father was Al Hajj Ibrahima Sory-Dara, almamy of Mamou. She was educated in Koranic and primary schools in Mamou, before continuing education in Conakry and

Dakar. She married aged 15 and had two children. In 1966, after divorcing her husband, she moved to Paris. There she pursued a successful career in fashion, married a Frenchman, and wrote her autobiographical novel.

Koumanthio Zeinab Diallo

Koumanthio Zeinab Diallo was born in 1956 in Labé, French Guinea, what is today known as Republic of Guinea. According to McNee (2003), Camara, O'Toole and Baker (2013) and Aflit Arts (2018), Diallo is a Guinean poet, novelist and playwright who writes in both French and Fulani. She has also worked as an agricultural engineer and in 2002 she and Bonata Dieng founded the Fouta Djallon Museum in Labé. Apparently, Koumanthio Zeinab Diallo has written so much in her lifetime and some of her works include the following:

- Koumanthio Zeinab Diallo, (2014). Les fous du septième ciel: Au-dela de l'excision (The madmen of the seventh heaven: Beyond circumcision). Silex/Nouvelles du Sud.

- Koumanthio Zeinab Diallo, (2007). Ngôtté-le-génie de la chasse - conte du Fouta Djallon en Guinée (Ngôtté the hunting genius - a story of the Guinea's Fouta Djallon). Paris: L'Harmattan.
- Koumanthio Zeinab Diallo, (2005). Les rires du silence (The Joys of Silence). Paris: L'Harmattan.
- Koumanthio Zeinab Diallo, (2005). *Les humiliées (Humiliated Women)*. Paris: L'Harmattan.
- Koumanthio Zeinab Diallo, (2004). *Daado l'orpheline et autres contes du Fouta Djallon de Guinée (Daado the orphan girl, and other stories of the Guinea's Fouta Djallon)*. Paris: L'Harmattan.
- Koumanthio Zeinab Diallo, (2004). *Le Fils du roi Guémé et autres contes du Fouta Djallon de Guinée (The son of the King of Guémé and other stories of Guinea's Fouta Djallon). With a preface by Bernard Salvaing*. Paris: L'Harmattan.
- Koumanthio Zeinab Diallo, (1999). *Comme une colombe en furie, poésie pour enfants (Like a dove in fury, poetry for children)*, éditions Linda.
- Koumanthio Zeinab Diallo, (1998). *Comme les pétales du crépuscule (Like Petals at Dawn)*. Lomé: La Semeuse.

Saïdou Bokoum

Saïdou Bokoum was born in 1945 in Dinguiraye, French Guinea, known today as the Republic of Guinea. Bokoum published a classic novel in 1974 titled *Chaîne*. O'Toole and Baker (2005) observed that the novel was about the plight of Africans living in France; and reported that he has published several works related to theatre. Moreover, Saïdou Bokoum is a Great Guinean writer of high reputation and scholarship articulation.

Tierno Monénembo

Thierno Saïdou Diallo – popularly known as Tierno Monénembo – was born in Porédaka in 1947 in what today is the Republic of Guinea. O'Toole and Baker (2005) described him as a Francophone Guinean novelist and biochemist. He was born in Guinea and later lived in Senegal, Algeria, Morocco, and finally France since 1973.

Essentially, Tierno Monénembo is one of the finest writers Guinea has and he has published eight books. Following potential excellence in his writing career, in 2008, he was awarded the prix Renaudot for *le Roi de Kahel* translated in English as The King of Kahel. In his narrations, Monénembo (2009) and Monénembo (2010) implied that:

> *In 1969, this son of a government official left Guinea, fleeing the Ahmed Sékou Touré dictatorship on foot to neighbouring Senegal. He then went to the Ivory Coast to pursue his studies. He went to France in 1973, again for his studies, and he obtained a doctorate in biochemistry from the University of Lyon. Afterwards, he taught in*

Morocco and Algeria. Since 2007, he has been a visiting professor at Middlebury College in Vermont, USA. Tierno Monénembo published his first novel in 1979. His novels often deal with the feebleness of intelligentsias in the African purviews, and the teething troubles of life and living of Africans who live in exile in the Republic of France. He is particularly interested in the history and connections of blacks with the forced immigrant diaspora in Brazil (Pelourihno). He recently devoted a novel to the Fula people and a fictionalized biography of Aimé Olivier de Sanderval, a French adventurer and explorer, originally from Lyon and Marseille (Pastré country), who admired their civilization and became a Fulani king. He uses the opportunity to revisit colonial history in order to bring this controversial period into the fictional imagination. He is currently working on the life of a Guinean Fula, a hero of the Resistance in France, executed by the Germans, as well as on the links connecting the black diaspora of the Americas with Africa. Tierno Monénembo was a writer in residence in Cuba when he learned that he was the 2008 winner of the Renaudot Prize. His award, however, put a spotlight on the growing place that French writers of African origin occupy in Francophone literature. It also emphasized, even if Tierno Monénembo lives in Normandy as if in the footprints of the Senegalese poet-president Leopold Sedar Senghor, that part of contemporary French literature is found in the South.

According to Monénembo (2010), the man Tierno was strong critic of the military coup d'état of 23 December 2008, in Guinea having brought to power the junta led by captain Moussa Dadis Camara, just after the death of President Lansana Conté, who led the country with an iron fist since 1984. Remaining relatively quiet in 2009, on both a political and literary level, until the massacre of more than 150 civilians by the army on 28 September in Conakry, he then wrote a column published in *Le Monde* entitled "Guinea, Fifty Years of Independence and Hell" to condemn these killings and call the international community to action.

Importantly, Tierno has man published works including the following:

- 2016 : *Bled*, Seuil
- 2015 : *Les coqs cubains chantent à minuit*, Seuil
- 2012 : *Le Terroriste noir*, Seuil — Prix Ahmadou-Kourouma, Grand prix Palatine
- 2008 : *Le Roi de Kahel*, Seuil — Prix Renaudot
- 2006 : *La Tribu des gonzesses : théâtre*, éditions Cauris
- 2004 : *Peuls*, Seuil
- 2000 : *L'Aîné des orphelins*, Seuil — Prix Tropiques
- 1997 : *Cinéma : roman*, Seuil
- 1995 : *Pelourinho*, Seuil
- 1993 : *Un attiéké pour Elgass*, Seuil
- 1991 : *Un rêve utile*, Seuil
- 1986 : *Les Écailles du ciel*, Seuil
- 1979 : *Les Crapauds-brousse*, Éditions du Seuil

Moreover, the Republic of Guinea has been endowed with very great and prominent writers that cannot easily be listed at once. Other prominent Guinean writers include the following:

- Ahmed Tidjani Cissé (born 1942)
- Alioum Fantouré (born 1938), economist and novelist

- Condetto Nénékhaly-Camera (1930–1972), poet and playwright
- Djibril Tamsir Niane (1932–2021), novelist and historian
- Lansiné Kaba (1941–2023), historian
- Mamadou Traoré, also known as Ray Autra (born 1916), teacher and poet
- Siré Komara (born 1991), novelist: *Mes Racines*
- Sory Camara, anthropologist
- Williams Sassine (1944–1997), French-language novelist

CHAPTER TWO

Problem of Human Rights Violations

Tires burnt during a clash on 13 April 2015 in the capital, Conakry, between policemen and Guinean opposition supporters. The protesters clashed with security forces over a dispute with the government over the timing of both local and presidential elections. During the often-violent protests, the security forces on numerous occasions used excessive force and engaged in unprofessional conduct, including theft.

Source: *Getty Images as cited by Human Rights Watch,* 2015

The entire world has 195 countries out of which 110 have experienced a peaceful demonstration at one point or the other in the history of those countries. A peaceful demonstration is a march or gathering, which people take part in to show their opposition or their support for something. Peaceful demonstrations are organized to vent out citizens' grievances that arise from the authorities' negligence for responsiveness; and in The Republic of Guinea, they have been staged due to agitations for repelling human rights violations and breach of democratic processes in the country.

Peaceful demonstrations are a powerful tool for political statements and are a constitutionally protected form of expression (Morales & Drury, 2019; Pen America, 2022). West African Network for Peace-Building – WANEP & Forum on Early Warning and Early Response – FEWER, (2000) admitted that the causes of peaceful demonstrations or protests include frequent electoral manipulations, arbitrary arrest and detention of opposition leaders, and economic deprivation. Scholars such as Lewis and Skutsch (2001), Chenoweth, Hunter, Moore, Olsen, & Reynolds-Stenson, (2017), Weissbrodt (2019), Schwie (2019), Amnesty International (2020), are of the opinion that among the causes of peaceful demonstrations, human rights violations, or abuse, though slow but steadily and persistently recurrent are paramount.

Essentially, government and authorities have geared efforts towards curtailing human rights violations of citizens, however, this doesn't seem to be enough. There is a need to investigate why peaceful demonstrations are staged and whether they have an impact on the reduction of human rights violations in the Republic of Guinea.

Paramount Duty of Government

The protection of the lives and property of citizens is enshrined in the constitution of every country of the world. The constitution of a country is a set of guidelines controlling or ensuring the regulations of the powers of its government and the rights and duties of its citizens. The paramount duties of government such as Government of The Republic of Guinea, according to Starck (2000) and Law Teacher (2021) is protection of legal interests of its citizens, which cover the interests of life, health, freedom, and property and also protection of some other interests and certain constitutionally recognized institutions. Beyond the protection of lives and property, the rights of citizens have been a principal target of governments. The fundamental rights and freedoms that belong to every person in the world, irrespective of gender, nationality, status, race, and religion are what constitute human rights. They are basic rights from birth until death and are based on common or universal ethics or values such as equality, dignity, and fairness. Essentially, the law defines and protects these potential values. Moreover, they are embedded in human rights charters or declarations; meant to foster equality in all fronts of life and living, especially in the modern generation of civilization and era of decolonization.

Researchers such as Abraham (2006), Prakash (2020), have lamented about the existence of human rights violations across the globe including The Republic of Guinea. Today, human rights and democracy are being challenged and put into question. While human rights have long been defended and promoted as a value in their own right, the evolution of global politics has increasingly shown that human rights abuses can also become "international security" issues and threaten the stability of the international system. For instance, terrorism can be fuelled by human rights violations. Migration flows are exasperated by refugees fleeing abusive governments. Failed states incapable of defending their own citizens can easily trigger civil wars and destabilize entire regions, with spill-over effects onto the global arena. Almost every day there are chilling instances of violence, ethnic cleansing, heinous torture, child abuse, manslaughter, and several other human rights violations. Despite the adoption of the Universal Declaration Human Rights (1948) and special covenants provided for the rights of children, women and disabled, crimes continue unhindered and unabated.

Human rights violations and abuses have been reported in The Republic of Guinea by Human Rights Watch – HRW (2011) when it noted that:

Since independence, Guinean presidents Ahmed Sékou Touré (1958–1984), Lansana Conté (1984–2008), and Captain Moussa Dadis Camara (2008–2009) have relied on ruling party militias and security forces to intimidate and violently repress opposition voices. Thousands of Guineans—intellectuals, teachers, civil servants, union officials, religious and community leaders, and businesspeople—who dared to oppose the government have been tortured, starved, beaten to death by state security forces, or were executed in police custody and military barracks. Other Guineans have been abducted from their homes and places of work and worship or gunned down as they demonstrated for better governance or the chance to freely elect their leaders. Their bodies have been hanged from bridges, stadiums, and trees, strewn across roads and meeting places, or simply disappeared without a trace. Countless Guineans were forced to flee their homeland. Guinea's judiciary, which could have mitigated some of the excesses, has been neglected, severely under-resourced, or manipulated, allowing a dangerous culture of impunity to take hold. As perpetrators of all classes of state-sponsored abuses and human rights crimes have rarely been investigated, victims have been left with scant hope for legal redress for even the most serious of crimes.

Essentially, it is in response to these human rights violations that global human rights and legal frameworks emerged to provide succor to abuse and violations such as United Nations Universal Declaration of Human Rights (United Nations, 1949), African Charter on Human and Peoples' Rights (ACHPR) (Organization of African Union, 1981),

Charter of Fundamental Rights of the European Union (European Union, 2000), and the Treaty of Lisbon (Mutua, 1999; Anno, 2014; Citizens Information, 2021 & Australian Human Rights Commission – AHRC, 2022). These legal frameworks on human rights provide the basis for the protection of fundamental human rights globally, including that of the people or citizens of The Republic of Guinea.

Nevertheless, despite global struggles to curtail human rights violations, governments and individuals continued to be accused of violation of peoples' fundamental human rights. This could be the reason why Amnesty International emerged; campaigning for a world where human rights are enjoyed by all (Amnesty International, 2022). Government's failure to protect the human rights of citizens has been reported by Boucher (2020), Darboe (2010), and Prakash (2020), suggest that this is why citizens resort to peaceful protests or demonstrations in order to seek for justice and reduction of human rights violations.

However, scholars or research organizations like World Peace Foundation (2007), Darboe (2010), and Carvalho (2011), lamented that despite continuous peaceful demonstrations in The Republic of Guinea, Guinea continues to be poorer and unstable, with frequent protests and mutinies. Since gaining independence from France in 1958, Guinea has experienced peaceful demonstrations despite some moves towards a more democratic system, including the adoption by referendum of a new constitution in 1990, bad governance, human rights violations, weak rule of law and impunity.

Essentially, if this is allowed to continue, there may be fears that The Republic of Guinea could become yet another failed state; moreover, the deadly consequences in the near future cannot be foretold. This is the reason that this research work comes in to assess the impact of peaceful demonstration on reduction of human rights violations in The Republic of Guinea.

Why Human Rights Violations and Peaceful Protests

This work is expected to be of benefit to Governments, Human Rights Activists, and researchers in general in the following ways:

1.   The work will make the National, Provincial and Prefecture governments aware of the laxity of government on the protection of the fundamental human rights protection of the citizens; and the need to strengthen it, which the study has recommended. It is non-protection of the citizens' fundamental human rights that result into peaceful demonstrations or protests. The results of the study and its recommendations will help the governments to take a drastic measure or decision on quickening its policies and actions on the protection of the fundamental rights of citizens of The Republic of Guinea.

2.   Moreover, it will benefit the Human Rights Activists by helping them to see the need of encouraging Pressure Groups to press more on Government, Policy Makers and Stakeholders to disembark informal corrupt policies that violate the fundamental human rights of citizens in The Republic of Guinea. The results of the study will acquaint the Human Activists with the details on types of human rights violations that prompt peaceful demonstrations and how they will come in to curtail the excesses of perpetrators of human rights violations or abuse in the country.

3.   In addition, the work will benefit private and university researchers by making use of the empirical evidence in their empirical reviews and related literature reviews.

Geographically, the work was situated in the Republic of Guinea. Contextually, it hinged on assessing Peaceful Protest or Demonstration and Human Rights Violations in The Republic of Guinea. It identified types of human rights violations that prompt peaceful demonstration, ways in which peaceful demonstrations can impact on reduction of human rights violations, factors militating against peaceful demonstrations to impact on reduction of human rights violations and strategies to be adopted to improve peaceful protests to impact on reduction of human rights violations in the country.

CHAPTER THREE

Conceptualization of Human Rights Violations and Peaceful Demonstrations

Image Source: *Global Pan Africanism Network*

Peaceful demonstrations or protests have existed globally since post creature before the antediluvian period in both domestic and public purviews. In the African climes such as the Tiv in Nigeria, Kissi in The Republic of Guinea, Akan in Ghana, the Mende in Sierra Leone, and Nande in Democratic Republic of the Congo, domestically, children staged domestic peaceful demonstrations by refusing to eat food until they received justice. Ovivehu (2021:9) admits the fact that peaceful demonstration or protest is a global phenomenon when he asserted:

> *Protest is a global phenomenon. Therefore, the past decade is saturated with instances of protests across the world, such as Occupy Wall Street, the Spanish Indignados, the first Arab Spring uprising of 2010 in Tunisia and Egypt, and the second Arab Spring in Morocco, Jordan, Sudan, Algeria, Egypt, Lebanon, Iraq, and Syria in the period of*

2018–2020. The Black Lives Matter movement, George Floyd and anti-lockdown protests were also carried out in various nations, such as the United States of America, Canada, Australia, New Zealand, and the United Kingdom, Italy, Spain, Germany, the Czech Republic, and other European nations. Similarly, the South American nations (Brazil, Ecuador, Chile, Argentina, Bolivia, Colombia, Peru, and Venezuela) also experienced widespread protests due to long periods of frustrations, dissatisfaction with the social policies of governments and mismanagement of the COVID-19 pandemic.

In Asia, common protests included the labour protests in China, the Anti-Extradition Law Amendment Bill movement in Hong Kong (2019–2020), the Candlelight Struggle or Candlelight Revolution of South Korea (2016–2017) and a host of others. In the African setting, common protests included protests related to the COVID-19 pandemic, the Fees Must Fall protest (2015–2016) and xenophobic protests in South Africa, the Malian spring protests of 2020, and the anti-third-term presidential bid protests in Ivory Coast in the run-up to the presidential election of 31 October 2020. In recent times, Ghanaians have also protested as a result of widespread socio-economic challenges, such as rising inflation, high cost of living, corruption and removal of fuel subsidies on goods and services.

Essentially, a peaceful demonstration is an act of expressing dissatisfaction without necessarily using a violent means. Mix (2014:3) and Teasley (2021) asserted that a peaceful demonstration or protest also known as nonviolent resistance or nonviolent action is the act of expressing disapproval through a statement or action without the use of violence. This type of protest has been used to advocate for a number of different causes, including human rights issues, anti-war campaigns, and expressing disapproval of various political/government policy issues. Some general methods include boycotting certain products, participating in a march or a sit-in, displaying a particular symbol, and handing out flyers. Moreover, a peaceful demonstration followed by violence may lead to demands for changes in police practices (Cambridge University, 2022).

According to Ministry of Interior (2010:6) and Castellot (2022:1), social uprisings that attempt to achieve social change through nonviolent methods are peaceful demonstrations and are not a new phenomenon, but researchers have so far not been able to determine the factors that lead to their success. Nonviolence is not a new phenomenon and has long been used by civilians across the world; there have been an array of waves of nonviolent civil movements. The term "peaceful demonstration" refers to a gathering or a march conducted by a group of people to publicly demand, protest, or express their sentiments, opinions or will by peacefully using various forms or means.

Peaceful demonstrations, sometimes called peaceful protests, arise basically due to human rights violations perpetrated against citizens, which makes them demonstrate with the aim of getting or seeking social justice. Soken-Huberty (2022) identifies some of the human rights violations that seem to likely prompt peaceful demonstrations or protests noting that:

> *A state commits human rights violations either directly or indirectly. When a state engages in human rights violations, various actors can be involved such as police, judges, prosecutors, government officials, and more. The violation can be physically violent in nature, such as police*

brutality, while rights such as the right to a fair trial can also be violated, where no physical violence is involved. Another type of violation is failure by the state to protect, which occurs when there's a conflict between individuals or groups within a society. If the state does nothing to intervene and protect vulnerable people and groups, it's participating in the violations.

Civil and political rights are also types of human rights violation that are violated through genocide, torture, and arbitrary arrest. These violations often happen during times of war, and when a human rights violation intersects with the breaking of laws about armed conflict, it's known as a war crime. Conflict can also trigger violations of the right to freedom of expression and the right of peaceful assembly. States are usually responsible for the violations as they attempt to maintain control and push down rebellious societal forces. Human trafficking is currently one of the largest issues on a global scale as millions of men, women, and children are forced into labour and sexual exploitation. Religious discrimination is also very common in many places around the world. These violations often occur because the state is failing to protect vulnerable groups.

Moreover, there are other types of human rights that are violated such as economic, social and cultural rights, which include: Contaminating water, for example, with waste from State-owned facilities (the right to health); Evicting people by force from their homes (the right to adequate housing); Denying services and information about health (the right to health); Discriminating at work based on traits like race, gender, and sexual orientation (The right to work); failing to provide

*maternity leave (protection of and assistance to
the family); not paying a sufficient minimum wage
(rights at work); segregating students based on
disabilities (the right to education) and forbidding
the use of minority/indigenous languages (the
right to participate in cultural life).*

Apparently, researchers such as Kennedy (2001:1);
Hubert, Weiss and Samkange (2001:144) and Maiese
(2003:2) asserted that there is now near-universal consensus
that all individuals are entitled to certain basic rights under
any circumstances. These include certain civil liberties and
political rights, the most fundamental of which is the right
to life and physical safety. Human rights are the articulation
of the need for justice, tolerance, mutual respect, and
human dignity in all our activity. Speaking of rights allows
us to express the idea that all individuals are part of the
scope of morality and justice. Moreover, to protect human
rights is to ensure that people receive some degree of
decent, humane treatment. To violate the most basic human
rights, on the other hand, is to deny individuals their
fundamental moral entitlements. It is, in a sense, to treat
them as if they are less than human and undeserving of
respect and dignity. Examples are acts typically deemed
"crimes against humanity", including genocide, torture,
slavery, rape, enforced sterilization or medical
experimentation, and deliberate starvation. Because these
policies are sometimes implemented by governments,
limiting the unrestrained power of the state is an important
part of international law. Underlying laws that prohibit the
various "crimes against humanity" are the principle of
nondiscrimination and the notion that certain basic rights
apply universally.

According to Gaikwad (2013:79), the number of deaths
related to combat and the collateral damage caused by
warfare are only a small part of the tremendous amount
of suffering and devastation caused by conflicts. Over the

course of protracted conflict, assaults on political rights and the fundamental right to life are typically widespread. Some of the gravest violations of the right to life are massacres, the starvation of entire populations, and genocide. Genocide is commonly understood as the intentional extermination of a single ethnic, racial, or religious group. Killing group members, causing them serious bodily or mental harm, imposing measures to prevent birth, or forcibly transferring children are all ways to bring about the destruction of a group. Genocide is often regarded as the most offensive crime against humanity.

Rather than simply killing off whole populations, government forces may carry out programmes of torture. Torture can be either physical or psychological and aims at the "humiliation or annihilation of the dignity of the person". Physical torture might include mutilation, beatings, and electric shocks to lips, gums, and genitals. In psychological torture, detainees are sometimes deprived of food and water for long periods, kept standing upright for hours, deprived of sleep, or tormented by high-level noise. Torture is used in some cases as a way to carry out interrogations and extract confessions or information. Today, it is increasingly used as a means of suppressing political and ideological dissent, or for punishing political opponents who do not share the ideology of the ruling group (Cassese, 1990:90, 123).

Human rights violations, when they are allowed to continue to meddle with the social ethics of citizens, can lead to peaceful demonstrations or protests, which is likely to lead to violent protests. This ensues, most likely due to potential difficulties that arise when those in power are responsible for human rights violations.

Peaceful Demonstrations and Reduction of Human Rights Violations

It is known globally that citizens increasingly turn to peaceful demonstration or mass protests in order to address grievances in the face of unresponsive elites, and these protests often drive significant changes in the political agenda and probably influence the rate of reduction of human rights violations. Davis (2015:4, 6) reported that:

When protesters or bystanders are harmed, democratic societies provide avenues for accountability and redress through the police themselves, the judiciary, human rights ombudsman offices, and local elected leaders. Yet too few of the abusers face serious repercussions. Seeking justice requires time and money, breaches of civic trust in the police are hard to rebuild, and physical injuries in some instances are beyond repair. A more immediate remedy is widespread public exposure of aggressive policing tactics, which reflect poorly on elected leaders and law enforcement officials. Mobile and web-based communication tools broadcast instantaneous revelations of bad behaviour, and the resulting public attention often bolsters support for peaceful demonstrators or protestors and puts pressure on the authorities to change course. In today's connected world, mass protests resonate far and wide. News travels quickly from the streets to the public, whether reported by traditional media, an official news source, or citizens directly. Consequently, it is a powerful weapon for changing public opinion. In a number of the case studies, governments and some opinion leaders used the media to attack the reputation and motives of the protesters. In 2011 we saw too many governments crack down in the name of restoring

*order when their citizens demanded universal
human rights and a voice in how they were
governed. These acts of repression triggered more
confrontation, more chaos, and ultimately greater
instability. The events of the year showed that the
real choice is not between stability and security; it
is between reform and unrest.*

Soken-Huberty, E. (2022) informed that in human rights treaties, states bear the primary burden of responsibility for protecting and encouraging human rights. When a government ratifies a treaty, they have a three-fold obligation. They must respect, protect, and fulfill human rights. When violations occur, it's the government's job to intervene and prosecute those responsible. The government must hold everyone (and itself) accountable. This doesn't mean that members of civil society don't also have a responsibility to prevent human rights violations. Businesses and institutions must comply with discrimination laws and promote equality, while every individual should respect the rights of others. When governments are violating human rights either directly or indirectly, civil society should hold them accountable and speak out. The international community also has an obligation to monitor governments and their track records with human rights. Violations occur all the time, but they should always be called out.

Freedom of assembly, and specifically for the purpose of demonstration or protest, is an issue in every state. Protests involve the rights to hold and express opinions and beliefs, to assemble peacefully, and to associate with others. Peaceful demonstrations or social protest and mobilization offer people the opportunity to petition the authorities in a peaceful manner and are natural channels for a wide range of legitimate complaints and grievances (Trascasas, & Casey-Maslen, 2014:3).

Peaceful demonstrations or protests occur in many contexts and are inspired by a highly diverse range of moral, religious, political, economic, social, and environmental concerns, among others. In recent times, very large demonstrations have been linked to economic, social, and political uncertainty and upheaval in many countries. These protests are often planned, but are sometimes more spontaneous (Lichfield, 2012). In societies that are experiencing economic hardship or political repression, protests are unavoidable. Peaceful protests should be understood as an expression of individual and collective freedom, which is essential to the exercise of personal liberty and vital to the life of a democracy. Importantly, Lichfield (2012) and Trascasas and Casey-Maslen (2014:4) imply in their reports that peaceful demonstrations are used as a means of curtailing or reducing human rights violations. A state that obstructs or prevents peaceful protests, deems them unlawful, or uses force to disperse or deters them, is not only violating the rights to freedom of assembly but also creating conditions that invite violence. It is in the state's own interest to ensure that protests can occur, and that they can occur peacefully. In prescribed circumstances, protests and assemblies may be dispersed, and in even more prescribed circumstances, may be dispersed by force. However, in many countries law enforcement officials are frequently accused of using excessive force against protesters. The use of force to disperse demonstrations has been attracting increasing international attention.

Researchers like Burnett (1986:252), Human Rights Watch (2007:14) and Onivehu (2021:9) believe that there are so many ways in which peaceful demonstrations or protests are staged such as strikes and boycotting. This has been witnessed across the globe including The Republic of Guinea. According to Gomez (2007), on 16 December 2006, Guinea's President Lansana Conté travelled to Conakry's central prison with his motorcade and personally secured the release of two close allies charged with embezzlement from Guinea's Central Bank, reportedly telling his entourage, "I am justice." The first, Mamadou Sylla, is alleged to be Guinea's richest businessmen and had been arrested at his home earlier that month in connection with his allegedly unlawful removal of millions of dollars from the Central Bank. The second, Fodé Soumah, former Central Bank deputy governor, was also arrested for alleged complicity in the affair. For the unions, who had "suspended" the 2006 strikes pending government economic reforms, the incident was the final straw. Several weeks later a new strike notice was issued. Citing executive interference in the affairs of the judiciary and the dire economic situation in the country, the unions called for an unlimited general strike as of 10 January 2007 until such time when there was a "return to the rule of law".

Gomez (2007) and Human Rights Watch (2007:13) reported that unlike the strikes of 2006, which focused almost exclusively on economic reforms, union demands in January 2007 were more overtly political, and included the nomination of a consensus prime minister with power to form a consensus government, review and renegotiation of certain mining, fishing and forestry agreements, and putting an end to corruption by prosecuting individuals charged with embezzlement of public funds. Burnett (1986:233), Lichfield (2012) and Trascasas and Casey-Maslen (2014:4) in their assertions imply that peaceful demonstrations advanced in strike actions and boycotting, public speeches, letters of opposition or support, declarations by organizations and institutions, signed public statements, declarations of indictment and intention, group or mass petitions, slogans, caricatures, and symbols, banners, posters, and displayed communications can be used in taming or reducing human rights violations.

Confusion is compounded by media usage. Media use the terms of "peaceful protest", "civil disobedience", and "protest" in an indiscriminate way. Fundamental rights of protest and expression can be viewed as falling within the baggage of the civil disobedience practitioner but as already indicated, while they may be legitimate tools in a civil disobedience exercise, they exist, to the extent that they do exist at all, in their own right to fight human rights violations or abuses (Burnett (1986:252).

It is important to know that previous researches, according to Capoccia and Kelemen (2007:341), Soifer (2012:1572), Bethke and Pinckney (2021:503), have shown that successful peaceful demonstrations or non-violent resistance (NVR) campaigns promote democracy compared with violent revolutions and top-down liberalization through public speeches, strike actions and boycotting among other measures. We consider democratic transitions as critical junctures where political actors' choices have an enduring impact on political development, and our main assertion is that democratic transitions initiated by peaceful demonstrations or protests have beneficial effects on post-transition democratic quality.

Factors Militating against Peaceful Demonstrations and Reduction of Human Rights Violations

The pitfalls of human consciousness or equality arise from corrupt life and living, most often from the political and economic bourgeoisie that lose self-consciousness due to selfishness, which ensues from greed (Agber, 2022). Humanity today suffers from this demeaning predicament that fosters human rights violations across the globe. Hussein (2015:4-5) brightens the citizens' hopes when he reported that:

> *In perhaps the most resonant and beautiful words of any international agreement, "all human beings are born free and equal in dignity and rights". The commitments made by all States in the Universal Declaration of Human Rights are in*

themselves a mighty achievement, discrediting the tyranny, discrimination and contempt for human beings that have marked human history. The Universal Declaration promises to all the economic, social, political, cultural, and civic rights that underpin a life free from want and fear. They are not a reward for good behaviour. They are not country-specific, or particular to a certain era or social group. They are the inalienable entitlements of all people, at all times, and in all places – people of every colour, from every race and ethnic group; whether or not they are disabled, citizens or migrants; no matter their sex, their class, their caste, their creed, their age or sexual orientation. Human rights abuses did not end when the Universal Declaration was adopted. But since then, countless people have gained greater freedom. Violations have been prevented; independence and autonomy have been attained. Many people – though not all – have been able to secure freedom from torture, unjustified imprisonment, summary execution, enforced disappearance, persecution, and unjust discrimination, as well as fair access to education, economic opportunities, and adequate resources and health-care. They have obtained justice for wrongs, and national and international protection for their rights, through the strong architecture of the international human rights legal system.

According to Trascasas and Casey-Maslen (2014:3) and Hussein (2015:4), the Human Rights Council has affirmed that "everyone must be able to express their grievances or aspirations in a peaceful manner, including through public protests without fear of reprisals or of being intimidated, harassed, injured, sexually assaulted, beaten, arbitrarily arrested and detained, tortured, killed or subjected to enforced disappearance". Although international human rights treaties do not recognize a 'right' to protest as such, it is generally agreed that the right to participate in protests is the exercise in concert of a number of rights. Specifically, the 'right' to protest depends on and exercises several rights that are at the heart of a democratic society, including freedom of peaceful assembly, freedom of expression, and freedom of association. The right to freedom of peaceful assembly is the logical point of departure for determining states' legal obligations with respect to peaceful protest. This right is guaranteed by international human rights instruments and has been interpreted by human rights bodies.

Despite global legal framework on human rights of citizens and the stringent fight by the United Nations, African Union, European Union and other potential human rights defenders or stakeholders, violation of the fundamental human rights of people worldwide has progressive zither on shrouded or lukewarm policies and inactions. Therefore, there are multiple challenges or factors that militate against the effective peaceful demonstrations or protests that helm human rights violators into slow tempo in perpetrating such violations or abuses on innocent citizens. In different countries in Africa and elsewhere such as The Republic of Guinea, there are trailing reports of the challenges facing peaceful demonstrators or protestors who seek for justice over human rights violations. In a report, Civicus (2022) narrated that:

> *The use of violence and the killing of demonstrators to disperse ongoing protests in Guinea entrenches impunity and is a major setback for the fragile transition, global civil society alliance CIVICUS said today. Human rights groups report that at least five people were killed and several injured as the armed forces in Guinea used violence to disperse protesters on 28*

and 29 July 2022. The protests were called by the Front National pour la Défense de la Constitution (FNDC) – a coalition of political parties, civil society groups and trade unions to demand for more transparency in Guinea's current transition and the establishment of an inclusive framework for dialogue. Following the protests, the authorities arrested human rights defenders Oumar Sylla, also known as Foniké Menguè and Ibrahima Diallo from the pro-democracy group Tournons la Page-Guinea (TLP) and FNDC and charged them with participation in a banned assembly, looting and destruction of property. Before the recent arrests several members of TLP and FNDC including Oumar Sylla were violently arrested on 5 July by the Repression of Banditry Brigade (BRB) while holding a press conference on the state of human rights and social and political situation in Guinea at the FNDC headquarters in Conakry, the capital. They were charged with contempt of court and disrespect for justice and later released.

Media or press restrictions, ethnic fractioning and arbitrary arrests, restrictions or detention have been identified by Childs and Fleming (2016:22) and European Union Agency for Fundamental Rights (2017:8) as some of the factors militating against peaceful demonstrations. Civicus (2021) reported that the Government of Eswatini has waged a brutal crackdown on peaceful demonstrators for democracy and economic justice. We demand accountability and support the demands for peaceful dialogue. Moreover, according to Ortega and Murillo (2018), since Wednesday the 18 April, organizations, networks, and human rights defenders in Nicaragua have been documenting and denouncing multiple violations of the right to hold peaceful demonstrations.

Some of the challenges or factors that militate against peaceful protests include: murders, disappearances, arbitrary detentions, physical aggressions, the use of stones, sticks, rubber bullets, tear gas, threats, acts of intimidation and the infringement of the right to information. Demonstrations were organized in response to the Government's imposition of the Social Security reforms that involve cuts of 5% in pensions, as well as other measures that affect the fundamental rights of Nicaraguan women and men.

Strategies Adopted to Improve Peaceful Demonstrations and Reduction of Human Rights Violations

Human rights violations or abuses seem to be what pushes citizens into a peaceful protest or demonstration. However, when citizens or people are not satisfied with how they are treated or government policies and treatments of the aborigines, and they resort to a peaceful demonstration or protest, the government, in most cases cramps down on them, a situation, which poses challenging posture. It is in response to the challenges that researchers suggest strategies possibly to be adopted to improve these peaceful demonstrations. Nassauer (2019:117) identifies such strategies as enhancing the flow of communication between peaceful demonstrators or protesters and police, ensuring clear territorial boundaries, and preventing rumours from spreading.

Human rights protection is an international concern and quite as such, Veuthey (1998:27) and Maiese (2003:3) asserted that international humanitarian law has been enacted to preserve humanity in all circumstances, even during conflicts. Such law "creates areas of peace in the midst of conflict, imposes the principle of a common humanity, and calls for dialogue". It rules out unlimited force or total war and seeks to limit the use of violence in the hopes of maintaining the necessary conditions for a return to peace. Various international committees are in place to monitor compliance with human rights standards and report any violations. When breaches do occur, they are brought to the attention of international tribunals or tried in an international court or war crimes tribunal. This is to say that seeking the attention of the international tribunals is one way of strengthening peaceful demonstrations to help foster protection of human rights of citizens across the globe.

Office of the United Nations High Commissioner for Human Rights (OHCHR, 2017:5) reported that protestors combined political and social demands, and sometimes addressed their claims to specific institutions. Due to increased repression by security forces, demonstrations in urban areas were combined with other forms of protest, including sits-in (*plantones*), blockades (*trancazos*), night rallies or pot-banging (*cacerolazos*). The risk of further deterioration of the human rights situation remains high, as the economic and social crisis remains dire and polarizing, political tensions continue to escalate OHCHR (2017:33) therefore, advocates ending violent repression of peaceful demonstrations, cease the use of excessive and disproportionate force, and suggests restricting the deployment of the security forces during demonstrations and preventing the involvement of security forces that do not have the mandate to exercise crowd control, as measures to improving peaceful demonstrations' aims.

Theoretical Considerations

In any intellectual society, all professional practices are expected to consider various intellectual frameworks aimed at advancing the attainment of goals and objectives of a given programme or research. They are intended to solve problems that arise in society or provide information for decision making of the government, policy makers or the stakeholders and authorities (Tita, 1991:17), Ugbagir (2014:62) and Igberadja (2015:11). This work apparently hinges on two theories: the Theory of Reasoned Action (TRA) and the Tiv Ancôgholuv Theory also known as the TAT.

Research is a process by which new knowledge is discovered. High-quality research is characterized by different attributes, many of which tend to be related to each other. In research, the interest in interpreting and describing how theory is built and how to call for explanations based on collected facts, measurements, and observations are of importance in understanding knowledge production. These two parts of conducting research are theoretical frameworks and methods, respectively. Moreover, a theoretical framework is the use of a theory (or theories) in a study that simultaneously conveys the deepest values of the researcher(s) and provides an articulated signpost or lens for how the study will process new knowledge. It represents relationships between existing findings that provide a conceptual and systematic organization for data about phenomena. The use of theoretical frameworks should seek to provide opportunities for scholars to discover their voice, along with intellectual resources, to build theories that seek to liberate, rather than control (Moore, Tuttle, & Howell, 1982:2; Georges, 2005:4; Salkind, 2012:26; Philipsen, 2018:13 & Nhan, 2020:1).

Apparently, Kumar (2011:15); Müller (2012:3), Grant and Osanloo (2014:12), Rudasill, Snyder, Levinson, and Adelson (2017:42) and Nhan (2020:2) asserted that the theoretical framework serves as the structure and support for the rationale of the research, problem statement, purpose, meaning, and research questions. The theoretical framework provides a foundational basis, or an anchor point for literature review, and most importantly, methodology and analysis. A study without a justifiable theoretical base is of "limited usefulness of findings and conclusions". High-quality research depends not only on structuring a 'network' of theories under investigation but also on developing, examining, verifying, and refining research methods. There are links between theoretical frameworks and methods, and they tend to reinforce each other. As a matter of fact, they are two sides of the same coin that cannot be separated.

Theory of Reasoned Action

The Reasoned Action Theory was propounded by Martin Fishbein and Icek Ajzen in 1967. According to Zarzuela and Anton (2015:85), Bernova, Indah, Heroza, Rachmadita, Septiani and Cahyan (2019:572), the Theory of Reasoned Action (TRA) suggests that individual behaviour is determined by the intention or intention to behave (intention) and that will, is a function of attitude (subjective) and norms (subjective norm).

Rogers, Archibald, Morrison, Wilsdon, Wells, Hoppe, Nahom & Murowchick (2002:886) and Trafimow (2009:502) stated that the theory derived from previous research in social psychology, persuasion models, and attitude theories. Fishbein's theories suggested a relationship between attitude and behaviours (the A-B relationship). However, critics estimated that attitude theories were not proving to be good indicators of human behaviour. The TRA was later revised and expanded by the two theorists in the following decades to overcome any discrepancies in the A-B relationship with the theory of planned behaviour (TPB) and reasoned action approach (RAA). The theory is also used in communication discourse as a theory of understanding.

Although Fishbein and Ajzen's theory of reasoned action has been a leading theory in social psychology for the last few decades, it also has been an object of criticism for much of that period and subject to definitional issues about what an attitude is (Trafimow, 2009:502). The theory of reasoned action (TRA or ToRA) aims to explain the relationship between attitudes and behaviours within human action. It is mainly used to predict how individuals will behave based on their pre-existing attitudes and behavioural intentions. An individual's decision to engage in a particular behaviour is based on the outcomes the individual expects will come as a result of performing the behaviour.

The primary purpose of the TRA is to understand an individual's voluntary behaviour by examining the underlying basic motivation to perform an action. TRA states that a person's intention to perform a behaviour is the main predictor of whether or not they actually perform that behaviour. Additionally, the normative component (i.e. social norms surrounding the act) also contributes to whether or not the person will actually perform the behaviour. According to the theory, intention to perform a certain behaviour precedes the actual behaviour. This intention is known as behavioural intention and comes as a result of a belief that performing the behaviour will lead to a specific outcome. Behavioural intention is important to the theory because these intentions are determined by attitudes to behaviours and subjective norms. TRA suggests that stronger intentions lead to increased effort to perform the behaviour, which also increases the likelihood for the behaviour to be performed (Azjen & Madden, 1986:545, Doswell, Braxter, Cha, & Kim, 2011:45, Colman, 2015:1, Glanz, Rimer & Viswanath, 2015:76).

According to Fishbein and Ajzen (1975:261), the Theory of Reasoned Action was propounded in 1967 and improved in 1975 to have adopted the following basic elements:

i.   Belief
ii.   Attitude
iii.   Subjective Norms
iv.   Intention and
v.   Behavior

Belief

Belief is the probability that an object has some attribute. Usually, this is used to mean that someone has a belief that some action or behaviour will lead to a consequence. Ajzen and Fishbein (1980) concerns were that the identification of the behaviour of interest and the development of the measures of intention, attitude, and subjective norm as sufficient to facilitate a general understanding of the determinants of behaviour; and recommended that belief-based measures could be used to provide more detailed information on the cognitive basis of behavioural choice. Fishbein and Ajzen (1975:261); Terry, Gallois and McCamish (1993:8) and Nickerson (2022) aligned to the necessity of incorporating salient beliefs, which are outcomes or referents into the belief-based measures of attitude and subjective norm. Hale, Householder, and Greene (2002:261) concludes that beliefs generally link some attribute to volitional behaviour or an attitude.

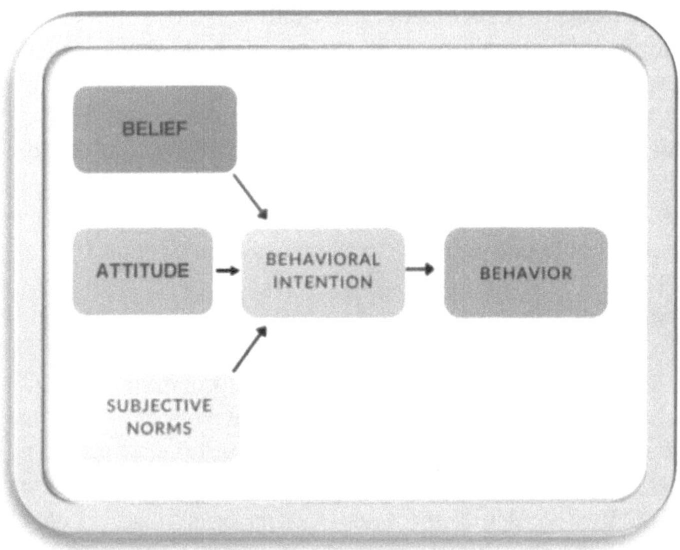

Figure 1: *Theory of Reasoned Action*

Attitudes

Fishbein and Ajzen (1975) define attitude as "a disposition to respond favourably or unfavourably towards some psychological object; and operationalize attitude as the person's evaluation of the target behaviour or, in other words, his or her feelings of favourability or unfavourability toward performing the behaviour". For example, someone who believes that smoking every day is bad for their health would hold an attitude toward smoking.

Attitudes are our progressive or regressive appraisal of a specific behaviour; whether someone thinks the behaviour is a good or bad idea, or if it will lead to outcomes, which they personally value. Tesser, and Shaffer (1990:481), Fazio (1990:75), Terry, Gallois and McCamish (1993:20) and Nickerson (2022) asserted that the main points of this model are that attitudes are a function of beliefs. Attitudes are equivalent to the sum of belief strength multiplied by outcome evaluation for each of someone's beliefs. For example, if a behavioural scientist wanted to predict someone's intention to exercise, that person's attitude towards exercise would be a function of all their beliefs about whether exercise will lead to the outcomes that they desire. If someone thinks that exercise will lead to desirable outcomes they will have a positive attitude towards it. Meanwhile, someone who thinks that exercise will lead to undesirable outcomes will have a negative attitude.

Subjective Norms

A subjective norm is a function of a normative belief and motivation to comply with the normative belief. This is the perceived expectation of important others regarding volitional behaviour. Motivation to comply is real or imagined pressure one feels for his or her behaviour to match the perceived expectation of others. Subjective norm is operationalized as the person's subjective judgement concerning whether significant others would want him or her to perform or not to perform the behaviour. As such, it represents a global judgement-across all salient referents of perceived pressure to perform the behaviour (Terry, Gallois

& McCamish, 1993:21; Hale, Householder & Greene, 2002:261).

Apparently, it is the submission of Fazio (1990:108), Kaur, Singh, Singh, and Singh (2017:242) and Nickerson (2022) that subjective norms are the sum of all the important people in someone's life and whether they think those people would want them to perform the behaviour. For example, someone may think of whether their spouse, doctor, or mother wants them to exercise. All in all, intentions are a function of attitude and subjective norms. Psychologists define two types of subjective norms: injunctive norms, and descriptive norms. Injunctive norms describe what people think other people think they should do. Someone who feels an injunction to carry out an action, such as eating acai bowls, does so because they think other people think that they should eat them. Descriptive norms, meanwhile, are someone's perception of what other people think they should do, though the truth may be different. For example, consider someone thinking about whether or not to wear a surgical mask. Their injunctive norm may be that they believe that most experts want them to wear a mask, as do their doctors and family members.

Behavioural Intention

Essentially, intention is the willingness to perform a behaviour. Alam, Jani, Omar and Hossain (2012:46) and Nickerson (2022) provide that this describes how likely someone thinks they are to perform a specific behaviour. Each of these terms is often treated by behavioural scientists as factors in an equation intended to predict human behaviour. As such, they are all related factors that ultimately contribute to behaviour. Alam, et al. (2012:47) asserted that behavioural intention is a function of both attitudes toward a behaviour and subjective norms toward that behaviour, which has been found to predict actual behaviour.

The central premise of the theory of reasoned action is that people make behavioural decisions based on a reasoned consideration of the available information. The theory can, therefore, be regarded as a deliberative processing model, to the extent that behavioral decisions are seen to be the consequence of the person's systematic consideration and deliberation of the information available to him or her. When deciding upon a course of action, the model proposes that people do not act spontaneously. But reflect upon the consequences of performing the behaviour, as well as their beliefs about what other people expect them to do. From this perspective, people are assumed to be "rational actors" (Tesser & Shaffer, 1990), who make reasoned behavioural decisions. (Fishbein & Ajzen, 1975; Ajzen & Fishbein, 1980:16; Fazio, 1990:77; Tesser & Shaffer, 1990:480; Terry, Gallois & McCamish, 1993:7 & Nickerson, 2022). Importantly, the Theory of Reasoned Action is related to this study.

The Theory of Reasoned Action is related to the work in that:

i.   Belief is the probability that an object has some attribute. Usually, this is used to mean that someone has a belief that some action or behaviour will lead to a consequence. The relationship is that this connotes the fact that citizens in The Republic of Guinea have a belief that human rights violation perpetrated against them by the government functionaries or violators will lead to a consequence.

ii.   Attitude is a disposition to respond favourably or unfavourably towards some psychological object; and attitude is a person's evaluation of the target behaviour or, in other words, his or her feelings of favourability or unfavourability toward performing the behaviour. The relationship is that this implies that citizens in The Republic of Guinea evaluate their human rights violations situation and deliberate on a target action, which is to stage a peaceful demonstration.

iii. Subjective norm is operationalized as the person's subjective judgement concerning whether significant others would want him or her to perform or not to perform the behaviour. Importantly, the relationship here is that the victim of human rights violations has a subjective judgement whether the fellow citizens would want them to carry out a peaceful demonstration against human rights violation against them or the government would prevent them from staging a peaceful demonstration.

iv. Behavioural intention is a function of both attitudes toward a behaviour and subjective norms toward that behaviour, which has been found to predict actual behaviour. The relationship here is that the intention of citizens or victims to stage a peaceful demonstration is found to predict the actual demonstration aimed at reducing human rights violations.

The Tiv Anchôgholuv Theory

The Tiv Anchôgholuv Theory also known as The TAT was propounded by Tim Cuttings Agber with Godwin Aôndohemba Fiase and Anthony Agena Igbashal in 2017. Bawa (2018:27), Akuha (2019:31) and Ape (2023:27) asserted that Tim Cuttings Agber, a Psychospiritualist and international research consultant co-propounded the theory with Godwin Aôndohemba Fiase who is a Doctor of Mathematics Education and Doctor of Measurements and Evaluation, and Anthony Igbashal Agena, a Doctor of Library and Information Science. The theory was published by one of the world's largest publishers of reputable research works, Lambert Academic Publishers in Germany.

According to Agber, Fiase and Igbashal (2017:47) the theory states that 'everything' must refrain from being aloof and must be grouped into classes where they belong by their own unique or agreeable characteristics for development. Researchers believe that the TAT is rooted from the Tiv astronomical principle and Agber (2017:430) and Bawa (2018:28) asserted that Tiv astronomical doctrine promulgates that the Anchôgholuv convey to the society the solidarity for purposeful compliments of wit for progressive strength of the vulnerable. This has anchored so many self-development parameters in the society among youths, women, and elders. In their arguments, Agber, 2011:51; Agber, 2017:431; Agber, et al, 2017:48) noted that:

> *The philosophy behind the idea of Anchôgholuv is to bring those who are feeble or weak in one way or the other together to collectively organize their minuscule strengths to achieve greatness. Confirmable facts in Tiv oral tradition and history as faceted in the work and war chant, which philosophizes Ayegher á Íkyon doo kwagh ga, Ayegher á Íkyon nande or ve. How realistic it is to have admitted that never underestimate the power of even weaklings when in their large groups. The essential part of the Tiv astronomical theory of Anchôgholuv teaches people to know who they are and where they belong in the Tiv society and promulgates that these people unite in oneness of purpose to change the face of their history in all circumstances. This goes similar in functionality with theory of Chameleonism, which*

promulgates the ability to adapt to a given situation favourable or unfavourable, at a given time and in a given way to get a given thing. I am not unaware that many have held and hold the opinion that events are controlled by fortune and by God in such a way that the prudence of men cannot modify them, indeed, that men have no influence whatsoever. Because of this, they would conclude that there is no point in sweating over things, but that one should submit to the rulings of chance. This opinion has been more widely held in our own times, because of the great changes and variations, beyond human imagination, which we have experienced and experience every day. The most powerful and perfect expression of the Tiv civilization through the medium of culture, growth, and progress must be traced to the promulgation of the Theory of Anchôgholuv. Nothing is better suited to lead the Tiv nation into an easy control of society than the aggravation of the Anchôgholuv Theory that ensures the illiteracy of the Tiv man is abrogated for civilization to ensue.

Shidi (2019:199) asserted that Tiv Anchôgholuv Theory was propounded by Tim Cuttings Agber, Godwin Aôndohemba Fiase and Anthony Agena Igbashal and the principle of Tiv Anchôgholuv Theory (TAT) provides the taxonomy, by which things must be and this can be understood as "classification of everything into groups" they belong for development. The TAT operates on the following principles:

1.   'Everything' encompasses humans and nonhumans in all knowledge, all skills and all behavioural tendencies.

2.   'Classification of everything' is the arrangement or ordering of 'things' (people, processes, ideas, skills, values, and functions) tangible or intangible into groups, based on some characteristics of those things.

3.   Characteristics of the things are not provided in a list of templates to be used but are available naturally or agreeably based on the knowledge that they exist to be classified.

Essentially, the Tiv Ancôgholuv Theory also known as the TAT is related to this study in that:

i.   The Theory provides that 'Everything' must refrain from being aloof. The relationship here is that victims of human rights violations refrain from suffering the human rights abuse alone but collect themselves together for a peaceful protest to curtail or reduce human rights violations in The Republic of Guinea.

Review of Related Studies

The work reviews the empirical studies that are related to this work in order to make sure that the work is not a duplication of a similar work, also to keep abreast of the current trend of related works to take the frontier of knowledge further.

Akiri (2013:1) carried out a study on students' and human rights awareness in secondary schools' environment in Delta State. The paper reviewed the concept of human rights, possible origin, and relevance to human society in general and the school system in particular. It evaluated people's level of awareness of these rights amongst students and teachers of secondary schools in Delta Central Senatorial District. The stratified random sampling technique was adopted to select the sample size of 150 students and teacher used for the study. The study adopted a descriptive survey design. The instrument used was the 3-scale questionnaire, designed by the researcher to collect data for the study. The simple percentage was used as a statistical tool for the analysis of data. The findings indicated, among others, that there is limited awareness of fundamental rights amongst secondary school students and teacher. The study recommended inter alia, that the state should seek to consciously promote fundamental Human Rights Awareness, by making the study of subjects which contains elements of the constitution as core, especially for those in the Primary and Secondary level of Education.

In another study, Eni and Arit (2016:38) investigated knowledge of education law and human rights violations among secondary school personnel in Nigeria. Two research questions and one hypothesis were answered and tested in the study. Survey research design was adopted, in which questionnaire was used for data collection. A sample size of 92 respondents were selected, using stratified random sampling technique from a population of 1,458 secondary school personnel, which comprised of principals, vice principals, compound masters and labour masters. A 17-item researchers' developed questionnaire known as "Knowledge of Education Law and Human Rights Violations Questionnaire" (KELHRVQ) was used for data collection, and data generated were analyzed using mean, standard deviation and t-test statistical tools at 0.05 significance level. The study found that secondary school personnel do not possess knowledge of the basic principles of law related to education. Again, secondary school personnel violate students' rights in schools in Nigeria. Conclusively, the study presumed that the extent of the violations of students' rights was contingent upon the ignorance of secondary school personnel of the basic principles of law related to education. Therefore, it was recommended that all education institutions (Universities and Colleges of Education) and programmes should incorporate legal aspects of education as a minimum curriculum requirement. Moreover, human rights violations should be curtailed to avoid violent protests.

CHAPTER FOUR

Analytical Discourse

Human rights violations have been lingering in The Republic of Guinea for quite a long time now. Therefore, collected data on opinions of respondents relating to human rights violations and peaceful demonstrations were analyzed. Based on the results of the analysis the discussion of the finding has implications as presented below.

Types of Human Rights Violations in The Republic of Guinea

A.   The findings in the first instance revealed that Police brutality such as torture, unlawful detention without trial and denial of bail to citizens, evicting people by force from their homes (the right to adequate housing), intentional extermination of a single ethnic, racial, or religious group (Genocide), discriminating at work based on traits like race, gender, and sexual orientation (the right to work), deliberate starvation of civilians for ethnic, political or religious reasons and unlawful sexual activity against the wish of the victim (Rape) are the types of human rights violations that prompt peaceful demonstration in The Republic of Guinea.

     This is in line with Stefan (2021:367) who admitted the existence of different types of human rights violations in The Republic of Guinea. It identifies the most significant atrocity risk factors and their indicators in accordance with the United Nations Framework of Analysis for Atrocity Crimes. It provides a taxonomy of measures, taken by a variety of external and internal stakeholders, in different combinations, which reduced the risk of atrocity crimes reoccurring after the 2009 stadium massacre in Conakry, Guinea. Moreover, United Nations Security Council (2009:376,377) lamented that the Guinean people have long been subject to coups d'états accompanied by grave and repeated violations of human rights. This situation is made possible by the existence of a very particular kind of army in Guinea and the repeated violations of human rights is a consequence of the impunity that is virtually institutionalized. These two phenomena—an atypical army and institutionalized impunity—are the real and profound weaknesses of the political system in Guinea. Stefan (2021:368,370) reported killing of protesters, raping of women by security forces and poor governance, and that Defense and Security Forces have a long history of gross human rights violations.

Human Rights Violations that Prompt Peaceful Demonstration or Protest in the Republic of Guinea

B.   The findings in the second instance revealed that widespread public exposure of aggressive policing tactics, which reflect poorly on elected leaders and law enforcement officials, mobile and web-based communication tools broadcast instantaneous revelations of bad behaviour, the resulting public attention often bolsters support for peaceful demonstrators or protestors and puts pressure on the authorities to change course, peaceful demonstrations or social protest and mobilization offer people the opportunity to petition the authorities in a peaceful manner, peaceful demonstrations are used as a means of curtailing or reducing human rights violations and promotion of democracy by peaceful demonstrations or non-violent resistance (NVR) campaigns are the ways in which peaceful demonstrations can impact on reduction of human rights violations in the Republic of Guinea.

Moreover, this is in line with United Nations Security Council (2009:2) and Stefan (2021:370) as their report noted that in response to the 2008 unlawful change of power, regional, sub-regional and international actors coordinated efforts to restore constitutional order in Guinea. The African Union (AU) and the Economic Community of Western African States (ECOWAS) acted swiftly, and together, they persuaded President Camara to agree to stand down from the presidency the following year and to allow for a transition to civilian rule. However, Camara eventually reneged on his promise and declared that he would run in the 2010 presidential elections, which led to an escalation in interethnic tensions and civilian protests to prevent human rights violations.

Challenges of Peaceful Demonstrations and Reduction of Human Rights Violations in the Republic of Guinea

C.	The findings in the third instance revealed that use of violence and the killing of demonstrators to disperse ongoing protests, arbitrary arrest of human rights defenders and peaceful demonstrators and unlawful detention, media or press restriction during peaceful demonstrations or protests, ethnic fractioning, unlawful use of teargas and rubber bullets by the police to dispel peaceful demonstrators and physical aggression, torture, forced disappearance and murder, are the factors militating against peaceful demonstrations to impact on reduction of human rights violations in The Republic of Guinea.

Apparently, this is in line with Camara (2000:311), Childs and Fleming (2016:22), European Union Agency for Fundamental Rights (2017:8), Stefan (2021:370) and Civicus (2022) who lamented that impunity is the norm; perpetrators of past violence and human rights violations have gone unpunished, including those responsible for massive human rights violations committed during the previous regimes of Sékou Touré and Lansana Conté. Peaceful protests or demonstrations that would have helped tame this faces a challenge of political biases, technical institutional barriers, because torture and crimes against humanity were not criminalized under Guinean law (which meant perpetrators risked being prosecuted for ordinary crimes). Furthermore, domestic law did not include command responsibility as a mode of liability, as required by the Rome Statute. Moreover, the use of violence and the killing of demonstrators to disperse ongoing protests in Guinea entrenches impunity and is a major setback for the fragile transition. Media or press restrictions, ethnic fractioning and arbitrary arrests, restrictions or detention are also some of the factors militating against peaceful demonstrations.

Approaches to Improve Peaceful Demonstrations and Reduction of Human Rights Violations in the Republic of Guinea

D.   The findings in the fourth instance revealed that enhancing the flow of communication between peaceful demonstrators or protesters, discouragement of the use of violence and the killing of demonstrators to disperse ongoing protests, ending of arbitrary arrest of human rights defenders and peaceful demonstrators and unlawful detention, provision of a policy to allow freedom of media or press during peaceful demonstrations or protests, stopping ethnic fractioning, preventing the involvement of security forces that do not have the mandate to exercise crowd control who unlawfully use teargas and rubber bullets to dispel peaceful demonstrators and prohibition of physical aggression, torture, forced disappearance and murder are the strategies to be adopted to improve peaceful demonstrations to impact on reduction of human rights violations in The Republic of Guinea. The hypothesis was rejected, and the implication was that there are significant strategies to be adopted to improve peaceful demonstrations to impact on reduction of human rights violations in The Republic of Guinea.

Essentially, this is in line with OHCHR (2017:33) and Nassauer (2019:117) who identify some strategies to be used in improving peaceful demonstrations as enhancing the flow of communication between peaceful demonstrators or protesters and police, ensuring clear territorial boundaries, and preventing rumours from spreading. Inclusive also is ending violent repression of peaceful demonstrations, cease the use of excessive and disproportionate force, and suggests restricting the deployment of the security forces during demonstrations and preventing the involvement of security forces that do not have the mandate to exercise crowd control, as measures to improving peaceful demonstrations' aims.

Conclusion

This book focused on how Peaceful Demonstration can help reduce Human Rights Violations in The Republic of Guinea. Scooping from related literature available, it was discovered that it is the human rights violations and abuse that prompt peaceful demonstrations. Important too, to note is the fact that having established the existence of human rights violations in The Republic of Guinea; and based on personal interviews conducted, Kikano (2022, in a verbal interview with the Author) said that "The Republic of Guinea has enshrined in its constitution provisions for the protection of the fundamental human rights of citizens; but authorities have refused to adhere to these provisions strictly. When we stage peaceful demonstrations, it is because our fundamental human rights have been violated but unfortunately, authorities push in the police against us to mete police brutality to dispel us from the demonstrations."

Moreover, in another oral interview, Doufangadouno (2022, in a verbal interview with the Author) said, "While we engage in peaceful demonstrations is to scare government, authorities or perpetrators of human rights violations so that they will desist from the abuse of our rights; but the authorities scare us with rapes, torture and arbitrary arrests to continue wallowing into the violation of our fundamental human rights." Therefore, it is concluded that there are significant types of human rights violations that prompt peaceful demonstration in The Republic of Guinea, and though there are ways in which peaceful demonstrations can impact on reduction of human rights violations in the country, peaceful demonstrations in The Republic of Guinea are plagued by so many factors that militate against it or overwhelming challenges.

Recommendations

There are factors militating against peaceful demonstrations to impact on reduction of human rights violations in The Republic of Guinea and therefore the following recommendations are made:

1.   In order to ensure that peaceful demonstrations have better impact on the reduction of human rights

violations, the flow of communication between peaceful demonstrators or protesters should be enhanced through advocacies and public awareness campaigns, which could be done by bills or jingles broadcast on radio and televisions stations across the country.

2.   The use of violence and the killing of demonstrators to disperse ongoing protests and ending of arbitrary arrest of human rights defenders and peaceful demonstrators as well as unlawful detention should be discouraged by strengthening of political will to enforce global and domesticated human rights treaties or laws.

3.   There should be a provision of a policy to allow freedom of media or press during peaceful demonstrations or protests, which will promote the ending of ethnic fractioning and prevention of the involvement of security forces that do not have the mandate to exercise crowd control who unlawfully use teargas and rubber bullets to dispel peaceful demonstrators and perpetrate physical aggression, torture, forced disappearance and murder.

Bibliography

Books

Abraham, M. (2006). *A new chapter for human rights: A Handbook on issues of transition from the Commission on Human Rights to the Human Rights Council.* Geneva, Switzerland: International Service for Human Rights.

Agber, T.C. & Agaigbe, G.T. (2023). *But I survived: An Authorized biography of Ambrose Pinne Iyortyer, Tor Kwande I.* Abuja: Konkofi (In Press).

Agber, T.C. (2011). *Fear – barrier to survival.* Abuja, Nigeria: TimeXperts Publishing.

Agber, T.C. (2021). *Impact of Tiv Religion on the prevention of the spread of Coronavirus disease among users in university libraries in Makurdi metropolis of Benue state, Nigeria (Research Monograph).* Abuja, Nigeria: Konkofi Publishers.

Agber, T.C., Fiase, G.A. & Igbashal, A.A. (2017). *Tiv Astronomy: information handbook.* Saarbrücken, Germany: Lambert Academic Press.

Ajzen, I. & Fishbein, M. (1980). *Understanding attitudes and predicting social behavior.* Englewood Cliffs, NJ: Prentice Hall.

Amnesty International, (2020). *Amnesty International Report 2020.* New York: Amnesty International Publications.

Ape, R. (2023). *Health information needs of Nigerians: An Integrative and inclusive approach to library services for national development (Inaugural Lecture Series No. 10)*. Lafia, Nigeria: Federal University of Lafia Press.

Banham, M. (2004). *A history of theatre in Africa.* Cambridge: Cambridge University Press.

Banham, M., Hill, E. & Woodyard, G.W. (1994). *The Cambridge guide to African and Caribbean theatre.* Cambridge: Cambridge University Press.

Boucher, A. (2020). *Defusing political crises in Guinea.* Washington DC: Africa Center for Strategic Studies.

Brooks, H.C. (1999). Conakry. In A. Appiah & H.L. Gates (Eds.). *Africana: The Encyclopedia of the African and African American Experience.* New York: Basic Civitas Books.

Camara, M.S., O'Toole, T. & Baker, J.E. (2013). *Diallo Koumanthio Zeinab. Historical Dictionary of Guinea.* Lanham, Maryland: Scarecrow Press.

Cassese, A. (1990). *Human Rights in a changing world.* Philadelphia: Temple University Press.

Castellote, M. (2022). What makes nonviolent resistance movements successful? (Bachelor Project). Linnaeus University, Sweden.

Charry, E.S. (2000). *Mande music: traditional and modern music of the Maninka and Mandinka of Western Africa.* Chicago: University of Chicago Press.

Colman, A. (2015). Theory of Reasoned Action. APA Dictionary of Psychology. Washington, DC, USA: American Psychological Association.

Conteh-Morgan, J. (1994). *Theâtre and drama in Francophone Africa: a critical introduction.* Cambridge: Cambridge University Press.

Emaikwu, S.O. (2015). *Fundamentals of research methodology and statistics (Rev. ed.).* Makurdi: Selfers Academic Press.

European Union Agency for Fundamental Rights, (2017). *Challenges facing civil society organizations working on human rights in the EU.* Vienna, Austria: FRA Publications.

Hubert, D., Weiss, T.G. & Samkange, S. J.T.M. (2001). The Responsibility to Protect: Supplementary volume to the report of the International Commission on Intervention and State Sovereignty. Ottawa, Canada: International Development Research Centre.

Hudgens, J. & Trillo, R. (2003). *The rough guide to West Africa.* New York: Rough Guides.

Kumar, R. (2011). *Research methodology: A step-by-step guide for beginners.* Los Angeles: SAGE.

Lewis, J.R. & Skutsch, C. (2001). *The human rights encyclopedia. Volume one (Eds).* New York: Sharpe Reference.

Machiavelli, N. (1999). *The prince.* (Translated with notes by George Bull and introduction by Anthony Grafton). London: Penguin Books.

Maiese, M. (2003). Human Rights violations. In G. Burgess & I. Burgess (Eds.). *Beyond intractability*. Colorado: Conflict Information Consortium.

Miller, C.L. (1990). Theories of Africans: Francophone literature and anthropology in Africa. Chicago: University of Chicago Press.

Mix, T. (2014). Lethal repression of peaceful protest in Africa: Why do (non-) accountable and military regimes shoot (Masters Student paper 15). Institut Barcelona Estudis Internationals, Barcelona, Spain.

Moore, G.T., Tuttle, D.P. & Howell, S.C. (1982). *Environmental design: Research directions for the Future*. Washington, D.C.: Environmental Design Research Association.

Nowrgu, B.G. (2006). *Introduction to educational research*. Ibadan: Longman Nigeria Publishers.

Onwudiwe, E. (2003). *Afro-optimism: perspectives on Africa's advances*. Westport, Connecticut: Greenwood Press.

O'Toole, T. & Baker, J.E. (2005). *Barry, Kesso Nene (1948–). Historical Dictionary of Guinea*. Lanham, Maryland: Scarecrow Press.

O'Toole, T. & Baker, J.E. (2005). *Historical dictionary of Guinea*. Lanham, Maryland: Scarecrow Press.

Pallant, J.F. (2007). *SPSS survival manual: a step by step guide to data analysis using SPSS for Windows*. England: Open University Press.

Salkind, N. J. (2012). *Exploring research* (8th Ed.). Upper Saddle River, NJ: Pearson Education, Inc.

Sankara, E. (2011). *Kesso Barry: autobiography, masculinity, ambiguity, and limited reception. Postcolonial Francophone autobiographies: From Africa to the Antilles.* Virginia: University of Virginia Press.

Shidi, H.J. (2019). *Compendium of theories for research: A Guide to developing theoretical framework.* Makurdi: Nats Printing and Publishing.

Trascasas, M.C. & Casey-Maslen, S. (2014). *Facilitating peaceful protests: Academy briefing no. 5.* Geneva, Switzerland: Geneva Academy of International Humanitarian Law and Human Rights.

United Nations Security Council, (2009). *Report of the International Commission on Inquiry Mandated to Establish the Facts and Circumstances of the Events of 28 September 2009 in Guinea,* UN Doc S/2009/693, 18 December 2009, pp. 2.

Book Chapters

Agber, T.C. (2017). Factors militating against the development of Tiv indigenous knowledge. In. P. Ngulube (Ed.). *Handbook of research on theoretical perspectives on indigenous knowledge systems in developing countries.* Hershey, PA: IGI Global.

Bekers, E. (2012). Barry, Kesso. In E.K. Akyeampong & H.L. Gates (2012). *Dictionary of African biography.* pp. 389–390. Oxford: Oxford University Press.

Falola, T. & Ter Haar, H. (2010). Introduction: Narrating war and peace in Africa. In T. Falola & H. Ter Haar (2010). *Narrating war and peace in Africa.* p. 1-18. Rochester: University Rochester Press.

Fishbein, M. & Ajzen, I. (1980). Predicting and understanding consumer behavior: Attitude-behavior correspondence. In I. Ajzen & M. Fishbein (Eds.). *Understanding attitudes and predicting social behavior.* Englewood Cliffs, NJ: Prentice Hall.

Glanz, K., Rimer, B.K. & Viswanath, K. (2015). Theory of reasoned action, theory of planned behavior, and the integrated behavioral model. In K. Glanz, B.K. Rimer & K. Viswanath (Eds.). (5th Ed). Health behavior: theory, research, and practice. San Francisco, CA: Jossey-Bass.

Hale, J.L., Householder, B.J., & Greene, K.L. (2002). The Theory of Reasoned Action. In J.P. Dillard & M. Pfau (Eds.). *The persuasion handbook: Developments in theory and practice.* London: SAGE Publications, Inc. Pp. 259-286.

McNee, L. (2003). Diallo, Koumanthio Zeinab. In S. Gikandi (Ed*.). Encyclopedia of African Literature, p.196.* London: Routledge.

Nassauer, A. (2019). How to keep protests peaceful. In A. Nassauer (Ed.). Situational Breakdowns: Understanding protest violence and other surprising outcomes. (*Oxford studies in culture and politics).* New York, USA: Oxford University Press.

Philipsen, K. (2018). Theory building: Using abductive search strategies. In P. Freytag & L. Young (Eds.). *Collaborative research design*. Singapore: Springer.

Terry, D.J., Gallois, C & McCamish, M. (1993). Theory of Reasoned Action and health care behavior. In D.J. Terry, C. Gallois & M. McCamish (Eds.). *The Theory of Reasoned Action: Its application to Aids-preventive behavior*. Oxford: Pergamon Press.

Journal Papers and Reports

Ajzen, I., & Fishbein, M. (1975). A Bayesian analysis of attribution processes. *Psychological bulletin, 82*(2), 261.

Akiri, A.A. (2013). Students' and human rights awareness in secondary schools' environment in Delta State. *Journal of Education Policy, 1* (1), 1-9.

Alam, S.S., Jani, M.F.M., Omar, N.A. & Hossain, T. (2012). Empirical study of Theory of Reason Action (TRA) model for ICT adoption among the Malay based SMES in Malaysia. *Business Management and Strategy, 3* (2), 43-53.

Azjen, I. & Madden, T. (1986). Prediction of goal-directed behavior: Attitudes, intentions, and perceived behavioral control. *Journal of Experimental Social Psychology, 22* (5), 453-474.

Bernova, N.M., Indah, D.R., Heroza, R.I., Rachmadita, T.A., Septiani, A. & Cahyan, R.D. (2019). Theory of Reasoned Action implementation on knowledge sharing process between alumni and college students. *Advances in Intelligent Systems Research, 171*, 572-580.

Bethke, F.S. & Pinckney, J. (2021). Non-violent resistance and the quality of democracy. *Conflict Management and Peace Science, 38* (5), 503-523.

Camara M.S. (2000). From military politization to militarization of power in Guinea-Conakry. *Journal of Political & Military Sociology*, 28 (2), 311–326.

Capoccia, G. & Kelemen, R.D. (2007). The study of critical junctures: Theory, narrative, and counterfactuals in historical institutionalism. *World Politics, 59* (3), 341–369.

Carvalho, A.L. (2011). *Republic of Guinea: an analysis of current drivers of change (Noref working paper).* Oslo, Norway: Norwegian Peace Building Center.

Chenoweth, E., Hunter, K., Moore, P., Olsen, T. & Reynolds-Stenson, H. (2017). Struggles from Below: Literature review on human rights struggles by domestic actors (Research and innovation grants). Working Papers Series. Denver, Co: University of Denver Press.

Davis, L. (2015). Overview: Mass social protest and the right to peaceful assembly. In L. Davis, S. Repucci, R. Raymond, & T. Rolance (Eds.). *Voices in the streets: Mass social protests and the right to peaceful assembly (A 12-Country special report).* Washington DC, USA: Freedom House Press.

Dinerstein, E., Olson, D., Joshi, A., Vynne, C., Burgess, N.D., Wikramanayake, E., Hahn, N., Palminteri, S.,

Hedao, P., Noss, R., Hansen, M., Locke, H., Ellis, E.C., Jones, B., Barber, C.V., Hayes, R., Kormos, C., Martin, V., Crist, E., Sechrest, W., Price, L., Baillie, J.E.M., Weeden, D., Suckling, K., Davis, C., Sizer, N., Moore, R., Thau, D., Birch, T., Potapov, P., Turubanova, S., Tyukavina, A., de Souza, N., Pintea, L., Brito, J.C., Llewellyn, O.A., Miller, A.G., Patzelt, A., Ghazanfar, S.A., Timberlake, J., Klöser, H., Shennan-Farpón, Y., Kindt, R., Lillesø, J.B., van Breugel, P., Graudal, L., Voge, M., Al-Shammari, K.F. & Saleem, M. (2017). An Ecoregion-Based approach to protecting half the terrestrial realm. *BioScience*. 67 (6), 534–545.

Doswell, W, Braxter, B., Cha, E. & Kim, K. (2011). Testing the Theory of Reasoned Action in explaining sexual behavior among African American young teen girls. *Journal of Pediatric Nursing, 26* (6), 45-54.

Eni, U.U. & Arit, M. (2016). Knowledge of education law and human rights violations among secondary school personnel in Nigeria. *International Journal of Education, Learning and Development, 4* (5), 38-47.

Esonwanne, U. (1993). The Nation as contested referent. *Research in African Literatures, 24* (4), 49-62.

European Union, (2000). Charter of Fundamental Rights of the European Union. *Official Journal of the European Communities, C* (364), 1-22.

Fazio, R.H. (1990). Multiple processes by which attitudes guide behavior: The MODE model as an integrative framework. *Advances in Experimental Social Psychology, 23*, 75-109.

Gaikwad, S. (2013). Human rights and violence in the society. *Journal of Current Science and Humanities, 1* (2), 79-83.

Grant, C. & Osanloo, A. (2014). Understanding, selecting, and integrating a theoretical framework in dissertation research: Creating the blueprint for your 'House'. *Administrative Issues Journal: Connecting Education, Practice and Research, 4* (2), 12-26.

Grantham, H.S., Duncan, A., Evans, T.D., Jones, K.R., Beyer, H.L., Schuster, R., Walston, J., Ray, J.C., Robinson, J.G., Callow, M., Clements, T., Costa, H.M., DeGemmis, A., Elsen, P.R., Ervin, J., Franco, P., Goldman, E., Goetz, S., Hansen, A., Hofsvang, E., Jantz, P., Jupiter, S., Kang, A., Langhammer, P., Laurance, W.F., Lieberman, S., Linkie, M., Malhi, Y., Maxwell, S., Mendez, M., Mittermeier, R., Murray, N.J., Possingham, H., Radachowsky, J., Saatchi, S., Samper, C., Silverman, J., Shapiro, A., Strassburg, B., Stevens, T., Stokes, E., Taylor, R., Tear, T., Tizard, R., Venter, O., Visconti, P., Wang, S. & Watson, J.E.M. (2020). Anthropogenic modification of forests means only 40% of remaining forests have high ecosystem integrity - Supplementary material. *Nature Communications, 11* (1), 1-10.

Human Rights Watch, (2007). Dying for Change: Brutality and repression by Guinean security forces in response to a nationwide strike. *Human Rights Watch, 19* (5), 1-64.

Kaur, P., Singh, M., Singh, K. & Singh, R. (2017). Exploring and predicting the antecedents of entrepreneurial intention of university students in Punjab. *Business Analyst, 38* (1), 240-255.

Krejcie, R.V. & Morgan, D.W. (1970). Determining sample size for research activities. *Educational and Psychological Measurement, 30*, 607-610.

Lederman, N.G. & Lederman, J.S. (2015). What is a theoretical framework? A Practical answer. *Journal of Science Teacher Education, 26* (7), 593–597.

Müller, S. M. (2012). The importance of clear methods descriptions in research papers. *Acta Paulista de Enfermagem, 25* (2), 3-4.

Mutua, M. (1999). *The African Human Rights Court: A Two-Legged Stool? Human Rights Quarterly, 21,* 342.

Office of the United Nations High Commissioner for Human Rights (OHCHR), (2017). *Human rights violations and abuses in the context of protests in the Bolivarian Republic of Venezuela from 1 April to 31 July 2017: Report by the Office of the United Nations High Commissioner for Human Rights.* Geneva, Switzerland: United Nations.

Onivehu, A.O. (2021). Causes, consequences and control of student protests. *Sociální Pedagogika | Social Education, 9* (1), 8-21.

Rogers, G.M., Archibald, M., Morrison, D., Wilsdon, A., Wells, E., Hoppe, M., Nahom, D. & Murowchick, E. (2002). Teen sexual behavior: Applicability of the Theory of Reasoned Action. Journal of Marriage and Family, 64 (4), 885–897.

Rudasill, K.M., Snyder, K.E., Levinson, H. & Adelson, A.J. (2017). Systems view of school climate: A Theoretical framework for research. *Educational Psychology Review, 30* (1), 35-60.

Soifer, H.D. (2012). The causal logic of critical junctures. *Comparative Political Studies, 45* (12), 1572–1597.

Starck, C. (2000). State duties of protection and fundamental rights. *Potchefstroom Electronic Law Journal, 3* (1), 1-51.

Stefan, C.G. (2021). Lessons in atrocity prevention: A Closer look at Guinea. *Journal of International Peacekeeping, 24* (3-4), 367-401.

Tesser, A., & Shaffer, D.R. (1990). Attitudes and attitude change. *Annual Review of Psychology, 41*, 479-523.

Trafimow, D. (2009). The Theory of Reasoned Action: A Case Study of Falsification in Psychology. *Theory & Psychology, 19* (4), 501–518.

Veuthey, M. (1998). International Humanitarian Law and the restoration and maintenance of peace. *African Security Review, 7* (5), 26-35.

Weissbrodt, D. (2019). Human rights conditions: what we know and why it matters. *Minnesota Journal of International Law, 28* (1), 1-53.

Zarzuela, P., & Anton, C. (2015). Revista Española de Investigación de Marketing ESIC Determinants of social commitment in the young . Applying the Theory of Reasoned Action. *Revista Espanola de Investigacion En Marketing ESIC, 19* (2), 83–94.

Internet Sources

Aflit Arts, (2018). Diallo Koumanthio Zeinab. Retrieved from www.aflit.arts.uwa.edu.au.

Agber, T.C. (2022). *Pitfalls of human consciousness.* Retrieved from https://twitter. com/TimAgber/status/1583213170738413569

Agber, T.C. (2023). *Colonialism or banditry?* Retrieved from https://www.linkedin.com/feed/update/urn:li:share :7134076628007014400/

Amnesty International, (2022). Who we are: where it all began. Retrieved from https://www.amnesty.org/en/who-we-are/

Anno, C. (2014). *The African Charter on Human and Peoples' Rights: how effective is this legal instrument in shaping a continental human rights culture in Africa?* Retrieved from https://www.lepetitjuriste.fr/the-african-charter-on-human-and-peoples-rights-how-effective-is-this-legal-instrument-in-shaping-a-continental-human-rights-culture-in-africa/

Australian Human Rights Commission, (2022). What is the universal human rights declaration? Retrieved from https://humanrights.gov.au/our-work/what-universal-declaration-human-rights

Bah, S. & Sienta, H. (2022). *Country: Guinea.* Retrieved from https://www.ifad.org/en/web/operations/w/country /guinea

Bariyo, N. & Faucon, B. (2021). Military faction stages coup in mineral-rich Guinea. *Wall Street Journal* (September 5). Retrieved from https://www.wsj.com/articles/military-faction-stages-coup-in-mineral-rich-guinea-11630866469

Burnett, R. (1986). *The right of peaceful protest in international law.* Retrieved from https://humanrights.gov.au/sites/default/files/HRC_assembly_Burnett.pdf

Cambridge University, (2022). *Examples of peaceful demonstration.* Retrieved from https://dictionary.cambridge.org/example/english/peaceful-demonstration

Central Intelligence Agency – CIA, (2022). The World fact book. Retrieved from https://www.cia.gov/library/publications/the-world-factbook/rankorder/2127rank.html

Citizens Information, (2021). *Charter of fundamental rights.* Retrieved from https://www.citizensinformation.ie/en/government_in_ireland/european_government/eu_law/charter_of_fundamental_rights.html

Civicus, (2021). Protest restrictions: Nearly 70 human rights groups condemn state violence in Eswatini. Retrieved from https://www.civicus.org/index.php/fr/component/tags/tag/protest-restrictions

Civicus, (2022). *Guinea: Release human rights defenders and lift restrictions on freedom of assembly.* Retrieved from https://www.civicus.org/index.php/media-resources/news/5955-guinea-release-human-rights-defenders-and-lift-restrictions-on-freedom-of-assembly

Darboe, A. (2010). Guinea (1958-present): Summary of events related to the use or impact of civil resistance. Retrieved from https://www.nonviolent-conflict.org/wp-content/uploads/2016/02/Guinea.pdf

Diallo, A. & Nossiter, A. (2010). Guinea votes in its first democratic presidential election. *New York Times* (November 7). Retrieved from https://www.nytimes.com/2010/11/08/world/africa/08guinea.html

Gilmore, E. (2020). EU action plan on human rights and democracy 2020 – 2024. Retrieved from https://www.eeas.europa.eu/sites/default/files/eu_action_plan_on_human_rights_and_democracy_2020-2024.pdf

Gomez, A.R. (2007). *Le millionnaire contesté, irrite les Guinéens en pleine crise sociale (Interview with Human Rights Watch interview with the then-serving Guinean Minister of Justice, Alsény Réné Gomez, Conakry, February 8).* Retrieved from http://www.lemonde.fr/web/article/0,1-0@2-3212,36-855908,0.html?xtor=RSS-3210

Human Rights Watch, (2011). *We have lived in darkness: A Human rights agenda for Guinea's new government.* New York, USA: Human Rights Watch.

Human Rights Watch, (2015). *Guinea: Security Force excesses, crimes - before elections, improve oversight, accountability, training.* Retrieved from https://www.hrw.org/news/2015/07/30/guinea-security-force-excesses-crimes

Human Rights Watch, (2022). *Guinea: Crackdown on right to protest threats to opposition freedoms as president considers controversial Third Term.* Retrieved from https://www.hrw.org/news/2019/10/03/guinea-crackdown-right-protest

Hussein, Z.R. (2015). *Introduction: Universal Declaration on Human Rights.* Retrieved form https://www.google.com.ng/url?esrc=s&q=&rct=j &sa=U&url =https://digitallibrary.un.org/record/815442/files/h uman-rights-booklet.pdf& ved=2ahUKEwirhMLuzu_6AhV1SvEDHVHpCH 0QFnoECAkQAg&usg=AOvVaw0GRCzDKSP-9qStrbq5hhC1

Internet Archive (1998). *Guinea-Conakry information. Retrieved from* https://web.archive.org/web/20090205044119/http ://www.uiowa.edu/~africart/toc/countries/Guinea-Conakry.html

Kennedy, H. (2001). *Conflict resolution and human rights-contradictory or complementary?* Retrieved from http://www.arrchre.com/publications/hrepa ck1

Larson, K. (2021). Explainer: Why is history repeating itself in Guinea's coup? *Associated Press* (September 7). Retrieved from https://apnews.com/article/africa-elections-senegal-west-africa-term-limits-4c595d69cbfd95d173b7ef1a6da0d5f8

Law Teacher, (2021). *Principles of a Legal Constitution.* Retrieved from https://www.lawteacher.net/free-law-essays/administrative-law/constitution-of-a-country-administrative-law-essay.php

Lewis, D. (2014). *Conakry, Guinea (1884-).* Retrieved from https://www.blackpast.org/global-african-history/conakry-guinea-1884/

Lichfield, J. (2012). *France: Huge gay marriage protest turns violent in Paris.* Retrieved from http://www.independent.co.uk/news/world/europe/france-huge-gay-marriage-protest-turns-violent-in-paris-8632878.html.

Ministry of Interior, (2010). *Implementation guide to the law on peaceful demonstration.* Retrieved from https://cambodia.ohchr.org/sites/default/files/Implementation_Guide-Rev_Eng.pdf

Monénembo, T. (2009). *La Guinée, cinquante ans d'indépendance et d'enfer (Guinea, fifty years of independence and hell).* Le Monde, 4 Octobre. Retrieved from https://www.lemonde.fr/idees/article/2009/10/03/la-guinee-cinquante-ans-d-independance-et-d-enfer-par-tierno-monenembo_1248904_3232.html

Monénembo, T. (2010). *The King of Kahel (trans. From French by Nicholas Elliott).* Seattle, Washington: Amazon Crossing.

Morales, S.P.J. & Drury, J. (2019). *Beyond peaceful protest: When non-participants support violence against the police.* Retrieved from https://www.researchgate.net/publication/336529947

Nhan, N.T. (2020). The role of theoretical framework and methods in research. https://www.google.com.ng/url?esrc=s&q=&rct=j &sa=U&url=https://osf.io/2x7vj/download&ved= 2ahUKEwjp3a-Hn_H6AhUk_7sIHRTrDPQQFnoEC AoQAg&usg=AOvVaw2O6g3ch6Jd53_8JHxn8ax q

Nickerson, C. (2022). *Theory of Reasoned Action. Simply Psychology*. www.simplypsychology.org/theory-of-reasoned-action .html

One World - Nations Online, (2022). *Nations Online: Guinea – Republic of Guinea – West Africa. Retrieved from* https://www.nationsonline.org/oneworld/ guinea.htm

Organization of African Union, (1981). African Charter on Human and Peoples Rights: Adopted by the 18th Assemble of Heads of States and Government, June 18th, Nairobi, Kenya. Retrieved from https://au.int/en/treaties/african-charter-human-and-peoples-rights

Ortega, D. & Murillo, R. (2018). *Joint statement: Dozens killed in Nicaragua by state repression of protest.* Retrieved from *https://www.civicus.org/index.php/fr/* medias-ressources/112-news/3151-joint-statement-dozens-killed-in-nicaragua-by-state-repression-of-protests

Paquett, D. & Timsit, A. (2021). Here's what we know about the unfolding coup in Guinea. *Washington Post* (September 6). Retrieved from https://www.washingtonpost.com/national-security/2021/09/06/guinea-coup-explained/

Pen America, (2022). *How to plan a peaceful protest.* Retrieved from https://campus freespeechguide.pen.org/resource/how-to-plan-a-peaceful-protest/

Prakash, B. (2020). Human rights violations – A Threat and curse to globe and humanity. Retrieved from https://www.researchgate.n et/publication/34649294 6_Human_Rights_Violations_Threat_and_Curse_t o_Globe_and_Humanity?channel=doi&linkId=5fc 4ff8d299bf104cf95c915&showFulltext=true#fullT extFileContent

Radio France International – rfi, (2022). *Guinea – Protests: Gunshots reported as demonstrators defy ban to protest against Guinea's junta.* Retrieved from https://www.rfi.fr/en/africa/20221020-gunshots-reported-as-demonstrators-defy-ban-to-protest-against-guinea-s-junta

Rédaction Africanews, (2022). *Violent clashes in Guinea's anti-junta protest.* Retrieved from https://www.africanews.com/2022/10/20/violent-clashes-in-guineas-anti-junta-protest//

Samb, S. (2013). *Guinea's Supreme Court rejects election challenges.* Retrieved from https://www.reuters.com/article/us-guinea-election-idUSBRE9AF0AP20131116

Samb, S. (2020). Guinea President Conde vows to tackle corruption during third term. *Reuters* (December 15). Retrieved from https://www.reuters.com/article /guinea-politics/guinea-president-conde-vows-to-tackle-corruption-during-third-term-idUSKBN28P27F

Schwie, H. (2019). *Examples of human rights violations.* Retrieved from https://borgenproject.org/examples-of-human-rights-violations/

Soken-Huberty, E. (2022). *What are human rights violations?* Retrieved from https://www.humanrightscareers.com/issues/what-are-human-rights-violations/

Teasley, D. (2021). Peaceful protest: Definition and examples. Retrieved from https://study.com/academy/lesson/peaceful-protest-definition-examples.html

The World Bank, (2022). The World Bank in Guinea: World Bank-supported projects in Guinea are focused in the areas of community development, rural infrastructure, education, transport, health, HIV/AIDS and more. Retrieved from https://www.worldbank.org/en/country/guinea/overview

Tita, J.M. (1991). An evaluation of national junior secondary schools social studies programme in selected JSS in Plateau State (Unpublished Doctoral Thesis). University of Jos, Jos, Nigeria.

United Nations, (1949). *United Nations Universal Declaration of Human Rights 1948.* Retrieved from http://www.jus.uio.no/lm/en/manifest/un.universal.decl aration.of. human.rights.1948.html

United Nations, (2021). Universal Declaration of Human Rights: History of the Declaration. Retrieved from https://www.un.org/en/about-us/udhr/history-of-the-declaration

West African Network for Peace-Building – WANEP & Forum on Early Warning and Early Response – FEWER, (2000). Policy Brief: Guinea-Conakry – Causes and responses to possible conflict. Retrieved from https://reliefweb.int/report/guinea/policy-brief-guinea-conakry-causes-and-responsespossible-conflict

World Atlas, (2022). *Ethnic groups of Guinea (Conakry)*. Retrieved from https://www.worldatlas.com/articles/ethnic-groups-of-guinea-conakry.html

World Peace Foundation, (2007). *African politics, African peace: Guinea short brief.* Retrieved from https://sites.tufts.edu/wpf/files/2017/07/Guinea-brief.pdf

World Population Review, (2022). *Guinea population 2022 (Live).* Retrieved from https://worldpopulationreview.com/countries/guinea-population

Unpublished Thesis and Dissertations

Akuha, M.T. (2018). The Impact of financial accounting on the development of 'Bam' among the Tiv people of Benue State (Research Project). Benue State University, Makurdi.

Bawa, A.R. (2019). Influence of Christianity on crime reduction among female adolescents in Makurdi metropolis of Benue state (Research Project). National Open University – NOUN, Nigeria.

Childs, G.D. & Fleming, R.J. (2016). Peaceful protest, political regimes, and the social media challenge (Master's Thesis). Naval Postgraduate School, Monterey, CA, USA.

Igberadja, S. (2015). Assessment of human and material resources for the teaching and learning of woodwork in Delta State Technical Colleges (Master's Dissertation). Delta State University, Abraka, Nigeria.

Interviews

Doufangadouno, M. (2022). Why do citizens of the Republic of The Republic of Guinea engage in peaceful demonstrations? (a verbal interview with Mano Doufangadouno, SOS Children's Village, Kankan, September 24).

Kikano, N. (2022). *What are the challenges facing peaceful demonstration in The Republic of Guinea?* (a verbal interview with Noel Kikano 53, Pharmacie Nouvelle Coronthie, Kaloum, Coronthie, Conakry, Guinea, September 27).

www.ingramcontent.com/pod-product-compliance
Lightning Source LLC
Chambersburg PA
CBHW031141250726
48655CB00002B/780